The Problem of Assessment in Art and Design

Edited by Trevor Rayment

Series editor: John Steers

intellect Bristol, UK / Chicago, USA

First published in the UK in 2007 by
Intellect Books, PO Box 862, Bristol BS99 1DE, UK

First published in the USA in 2007 by
Intellect Books, The University of Chicago Press, 1427 E. 60th Street, Chicago, IL 60637, USA

A catalogue record for this book is available from the British Library

Cover Design: Gabriel Solomons
Copy Editor: Holly Spradling
Typesetting: Mac Style, Nafferton, E. Yorkshire

ISBN 978-1-84150-145-1
ISSN 1474-6208

Printed and bound in Great Britain by The Cromwell Press

Contents

5 Acknowledgements

6 Preface

7 Introduction: The problem of assessment in art and design
Trevor Rayment

11 Chapter 1: The impact of formal assessment procedures on teaching and learning in art and design in secondary schools
Rachel Mason and John Steers

27 Chapter 2: Assessment in art and design in the primary school
Gill Hopper

41 Chapter 3: The assessment of GCSE Art: Criterion-referencing and cognitive abilities
Trevor Rayment and Brian Britton

49 Chapter 4: AS Level Art: Farewell to the 'Wow' factor?
Tom Hardy

59 Chapter 5: Striving for appropriate, reliable and manageable vocational assessment
Sylvia Willerton

69 Chapter 6: Portfolio development in a secondary teaching credential art program
Mika Cho

77 Chapter 7: (In defence of) whippet-fancying and other vices: Re-evaluating assessment in art and design
Richard Hickman

89 Chapter 8: Towards a more complex description of the role of assessment as a practice for nurturing strategic intelligence in art education
Leslie Cunliffe

107 **Chapter 9: Assessment in educational practice: Forming pedagogized identities in the art curriculum**
Dennis Atkinson

119 **Notes on contributors**

121 **Index**

Acknowledgements

I am much indebted to the authors: to those who have kindly allowed their papers to be reprinted here, and to those who have revised a paper or written a chapter specifically for this collection. There is little material reward for work such as this, but I hope the writers will be satisfied to have made an important contribution to our understanding of a somewhat neglected area of art and design education.

I am grateful to Intellect Books, Blackwell Publishing, NSEAD and the Editorial Board of *The International Journal of Art & Design Education*, who collectively have made this enterprise possible.

Finally, I should like to thank my colleague Fraser Smith for his forbearance, and my wife, Janet, and daughter, Sarah, for their endless support and encouragement.

Trevor Rayment

Preface

This book is the fourth in a planned series of anthologies dealing with a range of issues in art and design education. Titles published to date are *Critical Studies in Art & Design Education*, *Histories of Art and Design Education* and *Art Education in a Postmodern World*. The primary, but not exclusive, source of chapters are papers previously published in the *International Journal of Art & Design Education* and where appropriate these have been updated. It should be noted that any references to the English National Curriculum statutory Orders etc. are to that version of the curriculum current at the time of the original publication.

The National Society for Education in Art and Design is the leading national authority in the United Kingdom, combining professional association and trade union functions, which represents every facet of art, craft and design in education. Its authority is partly based upon a century-long concern for the subject, established contacts within government and local authority departments, and a breadth of membership drawn from every sector of education from the primary school to universities. More information is available at **www.nsead.org** or from NSEAD, The Gatehouse, Corsham Court, Corsham, Wiltshire SN13 OBZ (Tel: +44 (0)1249 714825).

John Steers
Series Editor

Introduction: The problem of assessment in art and design

Trevor Rayment

The procedures and purposes of assessment are not comfortably accommodated within the realms of art education. The constraints of an assessed curriculum and the consequent need to define practice that can be described as 'good', 'appropriate' or 'desirable' are anathema to many teachers of art and design. Arguably, there is a logical basis for art teachers' hostility, beyond their alleged instinctive resistance to regulation and conformity. Art is unique and therefore indefinable, and to attempt any kind of substantive definition would be effectively to deny options for creative progress or divergence. The questions and associated self-doubts that such assertions raise are not difficult to identify. How can one teach what cannot be defined? And, then, how can one assess what cannot be specified or taught? If then there is a problem with assessment in art and design education, the question of definition would seem to lie at the very heart of it.

In 1966 Ralph Smith wrote: 'Art education today is engaged in clarifying its conceptual foundations and in defining its relations to other disciplines of thought and action.'[1] Forty years on, it is still difficult to detect substantial progress in that process of engagement. There have been significant innovations to the school-based art and design curriculum during the intervening years, most notably the integration of critical and contextual elements within practice, and the introduction of criterion-referenced assessment, by which students' work is judged against a set of agreed assessment criteria or objectives. However, it is apparent from ongoing debate that art and design is still in need of a coherent and convincing rationale for its application in schools.

In order to dispel some of the confusion surrounding the subject, the discussion begins with a critical overview of the development of assessment in school-based art and design over recent decades. Rachel Mason and John Steers guide us skilfully through this recent history, and the reader is left in no doubt about the many conceptual and procedural inadequacies that have characterized 'progress'. The authors of this chapter were recently involved in a thorough and systematic review of published research on the impact of assessment on the secondary art and design curriculum. They found a scarcity of empirical research in this area, which may go some way towards explaining those perceived deficiencies, but such work as was relevant to that study, and, therefore, to this collection, is also set out concisely here in Chapter 1.

The next three chapters explore current issues of specific concern to the main phases of school-based art education. From an initial historical analysis, Gill Hopper develops a comprehensive account of the assessment of art at primary school level. The problem of definition is still apparent, and it is difficult to escape the conclusion that many of the perceived inadequacies of assessment in art are directly attributable to a failure to understand the form that a genuinely meaningful and creative art curriculum might take. The argument could be legitimately made that examination assessment objectives have themselves provided a definition of a kind. These given criteria are similar for all UK GCSE and A level examinations, and, on the face of it, they are clear enough and prescriptive enough to allow structured art and design courses to function and to enable some kind of assessment to take place. My own research (Chapter 3) tends to support the proposition that the criteria do indeed facilitate an objective measurement of performance. What this actually tells us in terms of students' creative achievements and whether it is helpful or appropriate is another matter entirely. Indeed, it is frequently argued that the school examination system's unbending insistence on conformity with common assessment criteria has led to the widespread adoption of predictable and orthodox approaches by teachers anxious to affirm their status, both in a curriculum that still embraces an implicit academic hierarchy and within the public arena of examination success. As a practising teacher, Tom Hardy is only too aware of the constraints and pressures placed on teachers and students by the current examination procedures, and in Chapter 4 he makes a passionate plea for a radical revision of these and, in particular, the controversial AS Level exam. Hardy's chapter gives us graphic evidence of the intensity of 'political' debate that may be engendered by arguments about issues that, to the outsider, must seem like the unexceptional detail of curriculum 'reform'.

GNVQ was intended to offer a high-quality alternative to GCE A Level, but its problematic development and eventual reorganization, discussed in Chapter 5 by Sylvia Willerton, provide a good illustration of some of the generic problems that have characterized formal assessment in art and design, as well as highlighting sensitive issues of parity between 'academic' and 'vocational' courses. It was always intended that portfolio evidence should comprise a major component of GNVQ and, indeed, several of the papers in this collection recommend the further consideration of portfolio work as a way forward in the quest for more effective means of assessment in art and design. In Chapter 6, a parallel, but distinctively American, practice of portfolio assessment is described by Mika Cho as she explores its effectiveness in evaluating the overall performance of trainee teachers. This chapter will be of particular interest to all trainee teachers of art, who will be at a stage in their professional development where, for the first time, they are forced to confront issues both of their own assessment and the assessment of their students. Whilst Cho's description of portfolio content may differ substantially here from a portfolio for recording or evaluating a practical art programme, the benefits offered to participating students and teachers are much the same, in terms of an objective authenticity and a renewed focus upon both summative and formative elements of assessment. The fundamental value of a formative approach is at the heart of home-grown proposals set out in the next two chapters.

Chapters 7 and 8 introduce two radical and imaginative proposals for rationalizing and rehabilitating the assessment of art. From a concise overview of assessment in its various forms, in Chapter 7, Richard Hickman develops an argument for an improved mode of assessment in art focused on an emerging picture of each individual's progress. Unlike the current procedures with their insistence on tight adherence to rigid criteria, Hickman envisages a central role in assessment for instinct or intuition, hence the unusual but apposite analogy with 'whippet fancying'. In Chapter 8, Leslie Cunliffe, too, is highly critical of established methods of assessing art and design. Many of these practices, he asserts, are inappropriate and educationally regressive. With reference to school inspection evidence,

Play

cognitive psychology and Wittgensteinian philosophy, Cunliffe makes the case for the construction of a paradigm of assessment in art that will lead naturally to self-regulated creativity and learning.

In Chapter 9, Dennis Atkinson draws on the work of Lacan and Derrida to illustrate a discussion of how students and teachers in the field of art and design education form their 'pedagogized identities'. Atkinson returns us to what, in earlier chapters, had become a familiar critique of the normative and essentialist tendencies of established assessment discourses. We are left with a plea for the valuing of difference and the singularity of practice and, throughout this chapter, with an implicit reminder, if such were needed, not only that the problem of assessment in art and design is still with us, but that it poses an intellectual challenge of some complexity.

There are persuasive reasons to accept that an effective, appropriate and agreed methodology for assessing students' progress in the subject is a worthwhile goal. But there are no practical, definitive answers in this book; indeed, each account of past or present procedures, and every proposal for change that is set out in the various contributions to this collection, itself reveals new problems for assessment in art and design. The argument for overcoming these challenges is simple yet compelling: unless we know where we currently stand, it is difficult to know where we need to go, and impossible to know what direction we should take. That applies both to curriculum content and to our methods of evaluating its processes and outcomes. It is to be hoped that the ideas discussed in these papers will contribute to a better understanding of the nature and purposes of art and design in education and to a more satisfactory and effective means of valuing it.

Notes and references

1. Smith, RA (ed.) (1966), *Aesthetics and Criticism in Art Education*, Chicago, Rand McNally & Co., p. vii.

Chapter 1: The impact of formal assessment procedures on teaching and learning in art and design in secondary schools

Rachel Mason and John Steers

Background: The context for GCSE and changes over time

The introduction in the mid-1980s of the General Certificate of Secondary Education (GCSE) marked the beginning of the 'reforms' that have continued unabated to the present time – not that the introduction of the GCSE was a rushed affair. The initial proposals to combine the General Certificate of Education Ordinary Level (GCE 'O' Level) and the Certificate of Secondary Education (CSE) examinations dated back at least to the days of the Schools Council and Prime Minister James Callaghan's seminal lecture at Ruskin College Oxford in 1976. The new examination was aimed principally at the top 60 percentile of the 16+ ability range although, in the case of art and design, the range was often much wider.

The GCSE examinations were welcome and overdue, marking the end of the perceived need for many art teachers to 'double enter' more able students for both examinations. Moreover, the rationale for the introduction of the GCSE was clear enough: the GCE/CSE system was incompatible with comprehensive education and, according to Her Majesty's Inspectors of Schools (HMI), work in secondary schools was dominated by examinations which, in their view, tended to govern the type and length of classroom activities. The reliability of inter-examination board standards then, as now, was considered questionable, so the new GCSE was administered by just four regional examining groups in England, one examination board in Northern Ireland and another in Wales. At the core of the proposals was the sensible aim to establish common national assessment criteria for all syllabuses and assessment procedures, to ensure that all syllabuses with the same subject title had sufficient content in common, and that all boards applied the same performance standards to the award of grades.

The members of the Secondary Examinations Council (SEC) GCSE Grade Criteria Working Party for Art & Design[1] recognized that the key to the whole exercise was how to define candidates' achievements through explicit criteria while not overly restricting the methods by which they might be achieved. The working party accepted that this approach involved many compromises. These included tacit agreement that it simply may not be possible adequately or equally to assess all curriculum objectives because the evidence for some of them may be too ephemeral to be valid. Lengthy consideration of the aims of art and design subsequently expressed in the GCSE National Criteria led to the identification of three equally weighted, closely interdependent and interrelated domains:

- a *Conceptual Domain* concerned with the formation and development of ideas and concepts;
- a *Productive Domain* concerned with the abilities to select, control and use the formal and technical aspects of art and design in the realization of ideas, feelings and intentions; and
- a *Critical and Contextual Domain* concerned with those aspects of art and design which enable candidates to express ideas and insights which reflect a developing awareness of their own work and that of others.[2]

Of course, this model is only one among many that could have been adopted and might have been equally coherent, but its conceptualization marked a significant step forward. As the working party struggled to develop the detailed criteria, a number of important issues emerged and significant lessons were learned. For example, the dangers of using adjectives such as 'simple' or 'sophisticated' in criterion statements because these kinds of words are ambiguous and open to diverse interpretations – a lesson that often has been overlooked in the interim as they increasingly find their way back into the assessment criteria lexicon.

In retrospect, the introduction of grade criteria was seminal in a number of ways. It can now be seen as the thin end of a wedge leading towards a state in which, as Eisner warns:

> *... infatuation with performance objectives, criterion referenced testing, competency based education, and the so-called basics lends itself to standardization, operationalism, and behaviorism, as the virtually exclusive concern of schooling. Such a focus is...far too narrow and not in the best interests of students, teachers, or the society within which students live.*[3]

From the mid-1980s, through successive agencies such as the School Curriculum Development Committee (SCDC), the National Curriculum Council (NCC), the School Examinations Council (SEC), the School Examinations and Assessment Council (SEAC), the School Curriculum and Assessment Authority (SCAA), to the present Qualifications and Curriculum Authority (QCA), governments have sought once and for all to 'nail the jelly to the wall' through repeated attempts to define the content, aims, objectives, assessment parameters and criteria for all subjects, including art and design. But analysis of the documentation suggests that there has been little new thinking and in reality much of this relentless process has consisted of 're-packaging' (repeated editing and précis) of previous documents to make them fit the common template currently favoured for all curriculum subjects. Thus the publication of Curriculum 2000 and the latest specifications for qualifications give the impression that all questions about what constitutes good practice in schools have been resolved. However, history is likely to prove that this is just an illusion – before long another perceived change of circumstances or belated admission of inherent problems are likely to require a further round of tinkering and reductionism.

Orthodoxy

For many years concerns have been expressed about an increasing orthodoxy of approach in art and design education as a consequence of the examination system. As early as 1982, Eddie Price, an experienced chief examiner and chair of the Schools Council 16+ art subcommittee, expressed concerns about the wash back of the examination system on classroom practice and prophesied problems with standardized assessment criteria:

> *The existing relationship between curriculum and examination syllabuses is a 'dog and tail' affair. The influence of external examinations has, to some extent, bred a species within the genus of 'School Art'. ...The question of whether the 'tail wagging the dog' is a satisfactory state of affairs must be linked with the possibility that the existing dog is a mongrel that defies simple definition. This is not to say that some mongrels are not healthier than some more easily categorised pedigrees, but it does make the establishment of national criteria guidelines more difficult – more difficult in the sense that criteria will necessarily be based upon generalisation of a plethora of objectives and practices – generalisation which will undoubtedly influence the future of art education.*[4]

In 1999, Norman Binch, one-time chair of the art and design panel of the largest examination board, reflected on how the GCSE, with its strong emphasis on 'process', influenced the style of work throughout secondary schools. He claimed that this frequently led to a single, linear classroom methodology where:

> *...the starting point is usually investigation and research, followed by the development of ideas and some experimental activities, and the completion of a 'finished' piece of work. Whilst the investigation and research can be into any relevant matters, including the work of artists, craftspeople and designers, or into concepts, issues and ideas, it is most commonly based upon objective drawing and visual analysis. The predominant sources of reference are collections of objects set up in the art room. The model reinforces the insular nature of 'school-art' and, even when reference is made to external sources; it is usually based on the same methodology of objective drawing and visual analysis.*[5]

This approach Binch describes has proved very reliable over the years producing 'safe' work that of its kind is often of undeniably high technical quality and on which teachers can depend for the award of good grades by the examination boards. Today the examination pressures in secondary schools are overwhelming and influence classroom practice not only at key stage 4 (15- to 16-year-olds) but throughout key stage 3 (11- to 14-year-olds). In our 'high stakes' education system it should be no surprise that teachers are adept at finding effective prescriptions for their students to follow that raise examination scores and, in turn, satisfy the various demands of league tables, inspection and threshold payments (a form of payment by results). But whether such a dominant conventional approach encourages real creativity and is in the best interests of pupils may be another matter.

How has this state of affairs come about? Since the early 1980s syllabuses have provided more and more detailed guidance. Typically, in the earlier generic GCE or CSE syllabuses, a few paragraphs sufficed to outline the content of an art and design examination course, but by 1999 separate art and design syllabuses of 20-40 pages were the norm. Twenty years ago syllabuses rarely contained specific aims, objectives, subject content or mark schemes – principally because the GCE 'O' level examinations generally were externally marked and it was not thought necessary to provide such information for teachers or candidates. There were marked differences between syllabuses but over time an ever-greater conformity between examinations boards/awarding bodies has developed, no doubt as a consequence of requirements to comply with the increasingly rigid examination specifications of the QCA and its various antecedents.

The earlier syllabuses included a wide range of optional papers with a focus in particular on fine art, design and craft skills; for example, lettering, photography, printmaking, pottery, theatre design and mural design. The number of students opting to pursue specialisms such as these in depth appears in general to have diminished, partly as a consequence of the decision to introduce the 'unendorsed' art and design examination and partly by the 'rationalization' of standard titles for endorsed papers.[6] By the end of the twentieth century the overwhelming majority of art and design candidates were entered for unendorsed papers although much of the work submitted took the relatively narrow form of drawing and painting.[7] It is clear that one consequence of the changes that have taken place has been that specialisms have been lost in many schools along with the real choice of studying a particular aspect of art and design in depth or following a more general course of study.

Not all the changes have had a negative impact. Positive outcomes include more guidance for students and teachers, improved student motivation and more examination time. For example, there has been a move away from question papers offering little more than one-word 'starting points' or instructions to examination supervisors about how to set up a still-life group or pose a model. Instead more recent question papers favour formats that offer more support for candidates, for example, a detailed design brief. Another recent approach is to provide a 'question paper' with a single common theme covering a wide range of art, craft and design activities that includes a long, discursive discussion of ideas candidates might wish to develop. Clearly, the intention is to motivate students to respond as creatively as possible to the required 'terminal test'.[8] Twenty years ago the time allocated for a terminal examination was often short, typically two to three hours in which to produce a drawing or composition. The time for all the examining groups is now around ten hours and there is a common pattern of question papers being issued to candidates some weeks in advance of the terminal examination in order to give them opportunity to research and plan their work.

Of particular significance is the marked trend away from an optional, formal art and design history element towards a general requirement for a 'critical and contextual studies' component.[9] This shift has been largely non-contentious but is not unproblematic. Pragmatism has played a part in the widespread acceptance of critical studies in secondary schools because the 'old' art history was very demanding of teaching time and only suited to reasonably academically minded pupils. In contrast, critical studies at examination level are often dependent on pupils researching the 'personal study' component of the examination in their own time.[10] The outcomes of this approach are varied with some exceptional projects in evidence. More generally, however, 'descriptive and non-contextual studies' might be a more apt title. Questions are in order, therefore, about whether or not pupils gain a coherent knowledge of art and design practice from independent 'research' that often has a narrow focus and encourages plagiarism accompanied by unproblematic pastiches of style. There is a continuing need to develop a clear rationale and assessment principles for the critical and contextual studies component in the GCSE and GCE examinations based on a more coherent view of content and cultural transmission, sound investigation, real critical thought and reaction, and articulate debate.[11]

Translating policy into practice

The past twenty years have seen a trend away from holistic assessment with no published criteria or mark schemes to a process of aggregation of component marks, based on mark schemes closely related to the published assessment objectives; and as a consequence of this examinations often determine the implicit taught curriculum. It is becoming evident that this leads to fragmentation and to teachers teaching to specific assessment criteria in the knowledge that so long as pupils provide clear evidence of some engagement with the ideas and practices embedded in the criteria they are rewarded, almost regardless of the actual quality of their work. Of necessity, assessment criteria are drafted so as to be generally applicable to a wide range of specialisms and activities. As a consequence they can be difficult to apply to some of the more unusual outcomes and inhibit some of the more creative responses to new media and technologies, for example, that reflect contemporary practice in art and design. In effect, when there is over-reliance on criteria they act as a regulatory device through which both teaching and learning practices are normalised.

Although 'coursework'[12] was not generally a component of the GCE 'O' level examination, it was a valued element of the GCSE from the outset. However, from the early1990s onwards the government has sought to reduce its importance in all subjects in favour of the terminal test (in art and design there is preferential treatment of the test and the permitted ratio of coursework to terminal examination is presently 60:40). What constitutes a 'unit' of coursework is not always well defined, although it is evident that the best and most committed candidates continue to select from a considerable portfolio of coursework.

Most of the change that has taken place has ostensibly been in the interests of increasing examination reliability. However, in art and design reliability remains an issue, particularly given the reduction in awarding bodies and much-increased size of entry for GCSE art and design examinations. In the past, smaller examination boards with relatively small entries employed small teams of examiners. Although not dependent on formal mark schemes or assessment criteria, it seems reasonable to assume that a good level of consensus used to be reached on standards, especially as one examiner often assessed all the work for a particular component. In 2000 at least one awarding body employed over 200 moderators and it is obvious that reliability must be dependent entirely on effective standardization procedures.[13]

Achieving accurate standardization presents a considerable challenge to the awarding bodies, but ever-tighter drafting of assessment criteria and rigid application may not be the answer. Boughton succinctly identifies the inherent problem:

> *...any attempt to use written statements intended to describe the range of complex and subtle characteristics of visual expressive work at any level of schooling will be less than adequate. ...The qualitative nature of the arts ...cannot be effectively captured in words alone. Linguistic representation of the arts is at best reductionist, and at worst misleading.*[14]

Common criteria have value in helping to focus the assessors' attention on particular concerns but they do not provide absolute measurement standards – assessment of the arts in schools still requires aesthetic judgement and connoisseurship based on experience of what pupils at a particular age can achieve. Moreover, criteria are written at a level of generality intended to accommodate any possible response. Clearly this only works when like is compared with like: anything more challenging that does not conform to the particular conceptual framework of the examination is less likely to be properly rewarded, thus encouraging further orthodoxy.

Developments since 2000

As part of the Curriculum 2000 reforms, in September that year the government introduced reformed General Certificate of Education Advanced Subsidiary and Advanced examinations (GCE A/AS levels)[15], together with new Vocational A levels and a key skills qualification. These were designed, it was said, to bring greater breadth to year 12 and 13 experience.

The new GCE A/AS level examination was divided into six units, each assessed by an external exam or coursework. The first three units of the A level make up AS level and the examinations could be taken at intervals during the course, or taken at the end of the two-year course. The introduction of modularity into the examination system created new issues for art and design. For example, a greatly increased workload for teachers and other more philosophical issues concerned with the 'wash back' of the examination on teaching and learning. Many art and design teachers in England and Wales responded to the introduction of these new specifications for GCE A/AS level examinations with concern. Correspondence on this issue was a regular feature of issues of A'N'D between 2001 and 2003[16] and Hardy's chapter 'Farewell to the "wow" factor?' in this book summed up many of these concerns, including the view that the modular approach tended to fragment teaching and learning.[17]

In addition to the wish to broaden 16–19 education, there seems to have been a government perception that the first year of an A level course was a time for relaxation and students' noses need to be kept to the grindstone. This view was mistaken. In art and design this was often a time for experimentation and trying out new ideas, when teachers supported student's individual creativity by giving them confidence to explore their own ideas and become less dependent on teacher-led projects. The new exam threatened this because every project, every piece of work from the start of the course needed to be fully realized and of the required standard. In effect, the central message was all too likely to be interpreted as 'don't bother being creative, avoid risks, play safe, do what is expected' – a view that if widely held would be damaging to students and the discipline.

PART 2

The case for basing policy on research

Nationally and internationally conflicting aims and values have always been in evidence in visual arts education. Thistlewood commented when he reviewed histories of art and design education over the past hundred or so years:

> *...it is difficult to ignore the obvious fact that fundamental, irreconcilable disagreements about policies, rationales and justifications have been usual. Revolution versus convention; child-centrality versus subject centrality; the expressive versus the utilitarian...*

In one sense these debates are the lifeblood of art and design. They should be encouraged rather than suppressed and, most importantly, ought to be informed by theory and whatever research evidence can be mustered – rather than the traditional but rather unsatisfactory English approach of engaging in some kind of *post hoc* rationalization and allowing gut instinct to drive curriculum and assessment design.

In 2002 the NSEAD Council formed a working party to prepare a discussion paper on the impact and effectiveness of formal assessment procedures in art and design and to make recommendations for development and change where appropriate. The hope was this would initiate constructive debate and address some key questions. For example, is a national structure for assessment in art and design necessary? Can a wholly objective standardized system of assessment ever be designed for art and design education? Is effective standardization possible? Do attempts to achieve this affect course content and teaching and learning styles for better or for worse? What do we wish to assess? Student capability? Student potential? Student attainment/achievement? 'Effective' teaching? Do prescribed criteria tend to fragment knowledge, skills and understanding? Can the language of criteria ever be sophisticated enough to encompass the possible range of creative visual and tactile outcomes? Should assessment be more holistic, authentic, negotiated? Is a 'terminal test' necessary? What does an examination assess that cannot be assessed through a coursework portfolio?

The NSEAD working party had just one meeting before the opportunity arose to bid for funds to support a systematic review of research into art education and assessment in collaboration with the Centre for Art Education and International Research (CAEIR) at Roehampton University, London. Subsequently, a number of working party members became involved in the review and the working party was adjourned pending the outcome of the review of evidence-based research reported later in this paper.

The evidence-based research movement

The Organisation for Economic Co-operation and Development's (OECD) review of Educational Research and Development in England[18] noted that the majority of research prior to the 1980s was promoted by organizations such as the Schools Council and the Assessment of Performance Unit and took the form of action research. During the 1980s, however, with the advent of the legislated national curriculum with published standards, aligned assessments, reduction of regulations for schools and accountability for results, government adopted the view that educational research and development was unnecessary. Continuous assessment and accountability were prioritized as mechanisms to ensure improvement. As a result few resources were provided for research or evaluation.

After a long period when it had been left to the universities, government turned its attention to educational research as a means to inform policy decisions. However, there was concern about the quality of existing research and how it was reviewed. By the middle of the 1990s it was becoming apparent that implementation of the educational reforms was more complex than anticipated and there was an effort to characterize teaching as a research or 'evidence-informed' profession.[19] Several reports found, not surprisingly, that connections between research, policy and practice were weak; that research was too supplier-driven and there was an emphasis on short-term evaluation at the expense of exploration and development. This led to research following, rather than leading, policy. It was noted that studies examining practice were small scale and unable to generate findings that could be generalized; that research findings were disseminated *ad hoc*; and that policymakers and practitioners often lacked the capacity to use research when it was available.[20]

Hillage *et al.*[21] recommended the development of a national education research framework. There was criticism of the method of research funding through the Higher Education Funding Council for England (HEFCE) on the grounds that it encouraged studies without potential for practical application and of no use to policymakers.[22] So the National Education Research Forum (NERF) was established in September 1999, to explore possibilities for greater collaboration between funders, to provide strategic direction for educational research[23] and to raise its quality, profile and impact within a national framework. The National Strategy for Systematic Reviews in Education (NSSRE) identified systematic reviewing as a move towards basing policy and professional practice on sound evidence of effectiveness. This approach had been developed by the partner Cochrane Collaboration and was already well established in knowledge areas such as health-care interventions, social policy, social welfare and criminal reform.

Thus the current interest in systematic reviews and evidence-informed policy and practice in education is part of a general move in the United Kingdom and elsewhere towards basing policy and professional practice on sound evidence of effectiveness. In contrast to traditional literature reviews, which typically examine a small part of the research evidence and take the claims of report authors at face value, systematic reviews aim to find as many studies as possible that are relevant to a particular research question and to employ transparent, explicit methods so as to identify what can reliably be said on the basis of these studies. Thus, systematic reviews aim to reduce the potential bias that is inherent in other approaches.

Evidence for Policy and Practice Information and Co-ordinating Centre (EPPI-Centre)

The Evidence for Policy and Practice Information and Co-ordinating Centre (EPPI-Centre)[24] is part of the Social Science Research Unit at the Institute of Education, University of London. It was established in 1993 to collate the results of public policy research in a format useful to policymakers, practitioners, academics and other research users. Its focus is on promoting systematic reviews of research evidence, developing methodologies for systematic appraisal of different kinds of research studies, and facilitating user involvement throughout the review and dissemination process. The Research Evidence in Education Library (REEL)[25], commissioned by the Department for Education and Skills in England, is the home website of the EPPI-Centre. This is a centralized resource with two main functions: to publish systematic reviews in education and to provide tools and databases for those wishing to undertake systematic reviews in this field.

The EPPI-Centre supports appointed external review groups by providing them with tools and techniques with which to carry out valid and reliable reviews of research evidence and to facilitate 'user involvement' throughout. A review question and methodology as described in a 'protocol' must be approved before reviewers locate and identify research reports using specialist computer databases as well as more traditional means. Reports are reviewed in an explicit and standardized manner so as to produce new and accessible synthesis of research studies for policy decisions and practice. As an important part of the synthesis process, reviewers assess the quality of the studies and assign weight to their findings. There is a manual outlining procedures for carrying out each stage of the review process. EPPI-Centre staff provide training in applying the method and carry out frequent quality checks. As is the case with any good research, making the review question and methods explicit in the 'protocol' before a review starts helps to reduce bias; for example, by ensuring that reviewers' procedures are not overly influenced by the results of the studies they find.

PART 3

The art and design review

The Centre for Art Education and International Research (CAEIR) at Roehampton University carried out systematic reviews for the EPPI-Centre in collaboration with the National Society for Education in Art and Design (NSEAD) from 2002 to 2005. Membership of the review group included art educators from four United Kingdom universities and experts from the Netherlands, Australia and the USA, together with 'user members' (art teachers, parents, a head teacher, examiner, art adviser and representatives of QCA and Arts Council England). A research assistant was appointed and small teams of researchers and users carried out the reviews on topics identified as significant policy and practice concerns using the guidelines and tools devised by the EPPI-Centre. A final report of the first review entitled 'The effect of formal assessment on secondary school Art and Design education: a systematic description of empirical studies' was published in September 2005.[26]

The review team[27] went through a formal application and registration process followed by a period of training by EPPI-Centre staff. The protocol (planning document) was peer reviewed and posted on the REEL website. It included a provisional research question, search terms for locating studies in indexes and databases and inclusion and exclusion criteria for screening them for relevance. Once this was approved, research studies were searched, identified, screened and key-worded to create an initial database.

The initial round of searching elicited 2,945 titles and abstracts. Of these, 2,837 had to be rejected because they were not on topic (not specifically about assessment or secondary school art and design), were not in English, produced prior to 1977 or did not constitute research.

Overall very few empirical studies of the impact of assessment on curriculum were located and inadequate reporting of important details of study methods and results compounded this difficulty. Eventually only eight studies by Atkinson (1998); Bennett (1989); Blaikie, Schönau and Steers (2003); De Eça (2004); McGregor *et al.* (1994); Rayment (1999); Sabol (1994); and Willerton (2001) met the inclusion/exclusion criteria.[28] They were duly subjected to key wording, which generated a preliminary descriptive map of this research. Then the reports were subjected to an in-depth data-extraction procedure (review) and the studies were assessed for quality and weight of evidence with respect to the review question. Unfortunately there was not sufficient consistent evidence to synthesize the findings and provide secure answers. Nevertheless, some indicative points emerged which merit further reflection and analysis.

The final report was published in the form of an extended map rather than a systematic review. It describes the eight studies in terms of their foci, contexts, aims, methods, samples and populations and data collection and analysis and the findings as reported by authors. Since the findings were not always substantiated by evidence that can be declared reliable or validated by comparative data the review team recommend caution in citing them.

Summary of the findings of the selected studies

Bennett's 1989[29] study of GCSE assessment in art and design found that teachers experience difficulty carrying out criterion-referenced assessment in spite of 'training'. Even when they were instructed to use the assessment objectives and grade descriptions they continued to draw on previous experience to recognize the standards they deemed necessary for allocating an appropriate grade. He observed them struggling to use the written word and exemplary photographs to assess student artwork. (He described the photographs as mere tokens or translations that failed to take account of significant constituents of spectator experience.) Bennett suggested that when examination boards use exemplar material as a way of illustrating the meaning of stated criteria they incur the risk of becoming prescriptive and creating orthodoxy; given that there is no finite definition of art, the process of art education must allow for idiosyncrasy, divergence and uniqueness. Bennett concluded that examinations tend to legitimate a particular view of art and that this is problematic.

Atkinson's 1998 study[30] was concerned with the discursive production of the pupil as a subject within the art and design curriculum and the hidden criteria that operate in assessment procedures. He found that the assessment discourse a group of teachers used to assess students' drawings of a chair was predicated on a perspectival paradigm of representation that therefore anticipated a particular kind of drawing form and, by implication, a particular kind of artist/drawer. He claimed that the teachers he observed did not assess the actual drawing ability of students, though this appeared to be the case, but rather they constructed, regulated and confirmed a particular kind of drawer within the pedagogic gaze of the assessment discourse. He concluded that assessment discourses do not identify prior abilities in learners but construct ability according to the terms of the discourse.

Macgregor *et al.*[31] studied arts assessment across Canada in 1994 and reported that it was used to *compare* students rather than as a measure of how well they accomplished certain tasks or skills. The data suggested that Canadian teachers were divided on the question of how or whether to reward *effort* in arts classrooms. The researchers also claimed that assessment practices sometimes work against socialisation – an important aspect of arts education in these researchers' view.

Rayment[32] studied art and design assessment and the requirements of the English National Curriculum for Art in 1999. Whereas he suggested that self-assessment is an important part of the formative process, he found that 11- to 14-year-old students tended to underestimate their own achievements, perhaps because of a sense of undue modesty. Rayment also identified problems with assessment of critical ability and concurred with Barrett[33] that the use of prescribed assessment tasks and criteria defined within limited parameters runs the risk of destroying that which they set out to assess – a reference to the problem of invalid or inauthentic assessment.

Sabol carried out a study of Visual Arts Achievement Tests from State Departments of Education in the United States[34] in 1999. From this he concluded that the test items examined did not adequately address the array of knowledge, skills and processes found in curricula. He reported that the limitations of achievement testing had caused some American states to consider introducing new assessment measures that they regarded as more 'authentic', alongside achievement tests, in the hope of establishing a more comprehensive measure of student learning. Sabol also referred to the possibility of bias in the tests he studied because not enough is known about how reading and vocabulary levels affect such test outcomes.

A more recent study of portfolio assessment carried out in Canada, The Netherlands and the United Kingdom by Blaikie, Schönau and Steers[35] in 2003 found some evidence of gender bias in assessment instruments in all three countries. The study found that males are less likely than females to know and understand the qualities a teacher looks for in their work. Males considered it less important than females to know and understand criteria for assessment and to discuss their art with their teachers. They understood group critiques of their work as less valuable than females. This may account in part for the continuing significant discrepancy between male and female achievement in the English GCSE and GCE A/AS level art and design examinations consistently reported by the QCA and Ofsted.

A study reported by de Eça[36] in 2004 set out to compare art and design examinations in England and Portugal and to evaluate their respective strengths and weaknesses. She found serious reliability, validity and utility issues in both systems but especially so in Portugal. She identified concerns about the authenticity of assessment and its impact on both teachers and students and its tendency to limit creativity and risk taking. Tension between curricula and external assessment was particularly evident in Portugal where it was said to produce negative wash back on the curriculum. An experimental examination based on a 'portfolio task' – trialled as part of this study – was found to be more authentic and also served to increase student and teacher motivation. Eça claimed it was possible to increase the validity of assessment by using portfolio-based tasks with no loss of reliability, but identified persistent problems of bias associated with student access to resources and the amount of advice teachers' offer them.

Finally, Willerton's[37] research into the development, distortion and subsequent dismantling of the more radical features of the General National Vocational Qualifications (GNVQ) Art and Design in England and Wales in 2001 sums up a number of key assessment issues. The teachers she studied reported an increase in student self-confidence, commitment, enthusiasm and motivation as a result of the increased independence in decision-making afforded by the GNVQ mode of assessment. But, at the same time, they viewed the emphasis on external assessment and large number of test instruments as obstacles to learning. Willerton reported that the documentation of evidence for assessment was excessive and time consuming. In what appears to be a clear case of assessment leading the curriculum, she concluded that recording evidence for assessment almost took on greater significance than the evidence itself.

Conclusion

There was disappointingly little empirical evidence in the studies to support the frequently conflicting claims that are found in the literature. A finding of the review as a whole was that research in art and design tends to be carried out for postgraduate degrees, is small scale, classroom-based and does not build sufficiently on previous studies.[38] Student initiated topics tend not to have their origins in a broader picture of ongoing research and the results are too limited to allow generalizations. Almost without exception, they leave many questions unanswered, relying on the possibility that other researchers might pick them up – something that seems to happen infrequently. The fact that most of the studies in the systematic map were practice based probably explains why they were small scale. But that this research takes place at all is indicative of some practitioners' desire for research evidence to guide them on these important matters.

The outcomes of the review do have a number of significant implications for the art and design field and for assessment in general. Allison[39] noted that science students are allocated research topics by their supervisors rather than left to identify them for themselves and suggested this is a better model of research training. It is clear that more reliable and valid studies of assessment are required. As a matter of some urgency, systematic investigations should be designed and undertaken of the impact of art and design examinations on curricula and, in particular, the extent to which external assessment dictates classroom practice. This concern has been discussed for far too long in the absence of any empirical evidence. It seems quite extraordinary that there appears to be no research in the public domain (if it exists at all) into the impact of examinations on the curriculum by any of the awarding bodies or by government agencies such as the QCA. Arguably such research should be undertaken by an independent body, such as the National Foundation for Educational Research (NFER), rather than QCA, and could include a comparison between assessment and classroom practices in each of England, Scotland, Northern Ireland and Wales. Important foci of such research would be to examine:

- The extent to which art teachers' pedagogical styles are test or examination-driven;
- How the resources available to art teachers influence what is taught and assessed;
- How different examination options influence teaching and assessment.

At the time of writing (winter 2005-6) the wider debate about the validity, reliability and purpose of public examinations and tests shows no sign of relenting in the wake of the 2004 Tomlinson report on qualification and curriculum reform.[40] There is recognition, even within the QCA, that public expectation of current tests and examinations is far in excess of their actual rigour and reliability. The tensions between formative and summative assessment remain unresolved. At the root of the problem is the difficulty, perhaps impossibility, of using the same assessment instruments for a range of frequently incompatible functions such as diagnosis, tracking, target setting, reporting, evaluation, selection, accountability and monitoring national standards. In response to the mounting evidence of the need for change, the QCA has called for a vibrant debate about curriculum and assessment issues[41] and the specifications for the GCSE and GCE examinations are once again under review.

In 2005 Ofsted continued to note the danger, evident in some schools, '...of the curriculum in the latter part of Key Stage 3 being little more than a preparation for the examination at Key Stage 4, with limitations placed on the breadth of study required by the National Curriculum in order to perfect a particular style of coursework associated with examination success'.[42] Katherine Tattersall, who retired recently as head of the Assessment and Qualifications Alliance, summed up the issues rather well when she warned that 'Professional confidence to teach a subject rather than just what an examination requires has plummeted. We are a nation obsessed by assessment, particularly external examinations'.[43] This is what needs to be changed.

Originally published in *The International Journal of Art and Design Education* 25. 2, 2006.

Notes and references

1. SEC, (1986), *Report of the Working Party: Art and Design Draft Grade Criteria*, London: Secondary Examinations Council.
2. *Ibid.*, note 1.
3. Eisner, (1985), *The Educational Imagination*, New York: MacMillan, p. 367.
4. Price, E (1982), National Criteria for a Single System of Examining at 16+ with reference to Art and Design, *Journal of Art & Design Education*, vol. 1, no. 3, pp. 397–407, Abingdon: Carfax Publishing.
5. Binch, N (1994), The Implications of the National Curriculum Orders for Art, *Journal of Art & Design Education*, vol. 13, no. 2, pp. 117–132, Oxford: Blackwell Publishing.
6. Examination specifications may lead to the general qualification title Art & Design (unendorsed) or to one of the 'endorsed' (i.e. specialisms) such as Art & Design: Fine Art; Art & Design: Three Dimensional Design; Art & Design: Photography; Art & Design: Graphic Design.
7. Downing, D & Watson, R (2004), *School Art: What's in it?*, Slough: NFER.
8. Terminal test – in art and design this is not a test in the usual sense but normally the final, summative or confirmatory examination unit. Often takes the form of an extended assignment that is externally set, internally assessed and externally moderated. Several weeks may be allowed for research and preparation but the 'test' consists of a defined period (say, 10 hours) for the candidate to work unaided under examination like conditions.
9. Examination specifications usually include a number of units and/or components – units are the smallest part of an examination or qualification that can be separately assessed; components are discrete assessable elements within a specification but which are not separately certificated.
10. Current specifications for art and design examinations in England and Wales can be accessed from URL: www.qca.org.uk.
11. For a discussion of these issues see: Hickman, R (ed) (2005), *Critical Studies in Art Education*, Bristol: Intellect Books.
12. Coursework – work completed during a course, typically an assignment, project or investigation, which is usually marked internally by the student's teacher before being moderated by an awarding body for moderation.
13. See, for example, various editions of the 'GCSE and GCE A/AS Code of Practice' published jointly by QCA, CCEA and ACCAC. The current 'GCSE, GCE, VCE, GNVQ and AEA code of practice 2005/6' is available from URL: http://www.qca.org.uk/13269.html. Accessed 14th January 2006.
14. Boughton, D (1995), Six Myths of National Curriculum Reforms in Art Education,. *Journal of Art & Design Education*, vol. 14, no. 2, pp. 139–152, Oxford: Blackwell Publishing.

15. GCE AS and A level examinations are usually taken by students aged 17 and 18 years respectively.
16. *A'N'D* (ISSN 1475-7486) is published by the National Society for Education in Art & Design (NSEAD). Correspondence on the examination system featured in a number of issues including: 1/2001; 2/2001; 9/2003; 11/2004.
17. Hardy, T (2002), AS Level Art: Farewell to the 'Wow' Factor?, *International Journal of Art & Design Education*, vol. 21, no. 1, pp. 52–59, Oxford: Blackwell Publishing.
18. OECD, (2000), Proceedings of CERI/OECD Conference, Lisbon.
19. Hargreaves, D (1996), Teaching as a Research Based Profession: Possibilities and Prospects, Teacher Training Agency Annual Lecture.
20. See for example:

    Tooley, J & Darby, D (1998), *Educational Research a Critique: Survey of Educational Research*, London: OFSTED.

    Edwards, J, Sharp, C & Benefield, P (2000), 'Systematic Reviews of Educational Research: Does the medical model fit'? Paper presented at British Educational Research Conference Cardiff University.

    Hillage, J, Pearson, R, Anderson, A, & Tamkin, P (1998), *Excellence in Research on Schools*, Research Report No, 74, London: HMSO.
21. Hillage *et al.*, *op. cit.*, note 20.
22. Bassey, M (2000), Reviews of Educational Research, *Research Intelligence*, vol. 71, pp. 22–9.
23. The National Education Research Forum (2000) was set up by the then Secretary of State David Blunkett in 2000. For the British Educational Research Association's response to this initiative and the consultation papers see their publication *Research Intelligence*, no. 74, into the impact of public examinations on the curriculum as taught January 2001.
24. For more information about EPPI visit URL: http://eppi.ioe.ac.uk/EPPIWeb/home.
25. The Research Evidence in Education Library (REEL) website of the Centre for Evidence-Informed Policy and Practice in Education can be found at URL: http://eppi.ioe.ac.uk/EPPIWeb/home.aspx?page=/reel/intro.htm.
26. Mason, R, Steers, J, Bedford, D, McCabe, C (2005), The impact of formal assessment on secondary school Art and Design education: a systematic description of empirical studies (online), *Research Evidence in Education Library*, London: EPPI-Centre, Social Science Research Unit, Institute of Education, University of London. Available from URL: http://eppi.ioe.ac.uk/EPPIWebContent/reel/review_groups/art/review_one/Art_rv1.pdf. Accessed 10th December 2005.
27. **Review Advisory Group:** Dr Dennis Atkinson, Lecturer Art Education, University of London (Goldsmiths College); Sheila Dowling, Senior Lecturer Art and Design, University College Northampton; Dr Richard Hickman, Senior Lecturer Art Education, University of Cambridge; Professor Rachel Mason (Director), Roehampton University; Dr Trevor Rayment, Course Leader PGCE Art and Design, University of Reading; Dr Paul Rinne, Deputy Head and Head of Art, Sheen School; Dr Dorothy Bedford (Research Officer), Roehampton University; Dr John Steers (Co-Director), National Society for Education in Art and Design; Dr Sylvia Willerton Education Consultant.

    International members: Dr Doug Boughton, Professor of Art Education, Northern Illinois University; Dr Lee Emery, Associate Professor, Arts Education, University of Melbourne; Dr Lynn Galbraith, Associate Professor, Art Education, University of

Arizona, Tucson; Dr Folkert Haanstra, Professor of Art Education, Amsterdam School of the Arts.

User members: Dan China, Association of Advisors and Inspectors of Art and Design; Melanie Fowke, art and design teacher, St Guthlac's School, Spalding; Dominic Harper, art and design teacher, Cowes Secondary School; Michele Kitto, art and design teacher, The Dragon School, Oxford; Nick McKemy, art and design teacher, Bacons College, London; Vivienne Reiss, Arts Council England; Robert Watts, primary teacher, Normand Park School, Fulham.

28. The selected studies were:
    i. Bennett, G (1989), Words in my eyes: the assessment of art and design in GCSE, Educational Studies, vol. 15, pp. 241–249.
    ii. Atkinson, D (1998), The production of the pupil as a subject within the art curriculum, *Journal of Curriculum Studies*, vol. 30, pp. 27–42.
    iii. Macgregor, R N, Lemerise, S, Potts, M, Roberts, B A (1994), Assessment in the Arts: A Cross-Canada Study, Vancouver: Visual and Performing Arts, University of British Columbia.
    iv. Rayment, T (1999), Assessing National Curriculum art AT2, knowledge and understanding: a small-scale project at Key Stage 3, *Journal of Art and Design Education*, vol. 18, pp 189–194.
    v. Sabol, F R (1994), A critical examination of visual arts achievement tests from State Departments of Education in the United States, unpublished Ph.D. thesis, Bloomington: Indiana University.
    vi. Blaikie, F, Schönau, D, Steers, J (2003), Students' gendered experiences of art portfolio assessment in Canada, The Netherlands and England, *Studies in Art Education*, vol. 44, pp. 335–349.
    vii. de Eça, M T (2004), Developing a new conceptual framework for pre-university art examinations in Portugal, unpublished Ph.D. thesis, Roehampton University, London.
    viii. Willerton, S (2001), GNVQ art and design: the development, distortion and subsequent dismantling of its more radical features, unpublished Ph.D. thesis, Brighton: University of Sussex.
29. *Ibid.*, note 28 (i).
30. *Ibid.*, note 28 (ii).
31. *Ibid.*, note 28(iii).
32. *Ibid.*, note 28(iv).
33. Barrett, M (1979), *Art Education: A Strategy for Course Design*, London, Heinemann Educational Books, pp. 55–59.
34. *Ibid.*, note 28(v).
35. *Ibid.*, note 28 (vi).
36. *Ibid.* note 28 (vii).
37. *Ibid.*, note 28 (viii).
38. Zimmerman, E (ed.) (1999), *Creating a Visual Arts Agenda Towards the 21st Century*, NAEA Commission on Research in Art Education Status Reports, Reston, Virginia: NAEA.
39. Allison, B (1988), *Research in Art and Design: Research problems, Programmes and Data Bases*, unpublished conference paper, London: Central School of Art and Design.

40. Working Group on 14-19 Reform (2004) 14-19 Qualification and Curriculum Reform: Final report (online) London: Department for Education and Skills. Available from URL: http://www.14-19reform.gov.uk. Accessed 15th October 2005.
41. See, for example, the QCA Futures website at URL: http://www.qca.org.uk/11232.html.
42. Ofsted, (2005), Ofsted subject reports 2003/04: Art & design in secondary schools (online). Available from URL: http://www.ofsted.gov.uk/publications/annualreport 0304/subject_report (Accessed 14th April 2005)
43. Tattersall, K (2003), A National Obsession, Guardian Education, 30th September, p. 4.

Chapter 2: Assessment in art and design in the primary school

Gill Hopper

The assessment of children's art and design work in the primary classroom, whether at Foundation Stage, Key Stage 1 or Key Stage 2, is a difficult issue that is often only superficially addressed in books on art education and even in the National Curriculum for Art and Design itself. For many primary teachers it is therefore an area which remains unresolved. In my experience, primary trainee teachers are particularly anxious about how to assess children's artwork and expect to be provided with a set of foolproof criteria upon which their judgements might be based. Since all children bring their own personal perspective and experience to bear upon their artwork and, according to the type of activity, operate both conceptually and physically (in terms of hand-eye coordination) in different ways and at varying levels, the answer to such a request is not straightforward.

For primary trainees who may have dropped art as one of their secondary school subjects around year 9, it is especially difficult to assess children's art confidently and appropriately. Many have no measure of their own artistic talents and potential – unless related to their (in)ability to draw accurately. It is not enough, as some might suggest, simply to identify how well the aims and objectives of the art and design lesson were met, as this in effect says more about the ability of the teacher and the appropriateness of the activity, than it does about the artistic ability of the child.

Art specialist primary trainees appear much less concerned about the issue of assessment. This clearly relates to their familiarity with the various media, their confidence in handling a range of materials, and their understanding of the properties of those materials. As artists themselves they understand the technicalities of making art and the frustrations experienced when a particular medium or material does not respond or perform as expected. Their understanding of what is 'good' art and design is also significantly further developed. However, it is still not easy for such students to actually relate their own experience to the developing and individual artwork of children, especially to work of a more spontaneous self-expressive kind, so that any form of assessment is both insightful and fair (also workable and transferable).

Some historical perspectives

Art and design education in the primary classroom has changed significantly over the last hundred years and its history might be described as a pendulum swinging backwards and forwards. To have some understanding of those changes and developments may help to appreciate why the issue of art assessment is not straightforward.

Today primary classroom art is largely driven by the requirements of The National Curriculum for Art and Design (1999)[1] and enhanced or underpinned by the QCA (2000) scheme of work.[2] It will be helpful here to understand the origins of its development. One hundred years ago, at the turn of the twentieth century, the disciplined drawing exercises of the elementary school (complete with attainments and payment-by-results policies) and their link to design and manufacturing were slowly being abandoned in favour of a more child-centred approach. With the advent of Modernism, modern views of childhood and the notion of 'Child Art' had begun to emerge. By the 1930s teachers were significantly influenced by the work and beliefs of a growing band of art educationalists, in particular Marion Richardson. Richardson, an advocate of the Viennese artist Franz Cizek's pioneering work with children[3], promoted the then radical view that children's drawings should be recognized as aesthetically pleasing in their own right and not be considered as poor adult art. Her use of mental visualization, based on verbal descriptions to stimulate the imagination (known as 'mind' or 'word pictures'), and simple pattern making with the new hog-hair brushes and powder paint, was to transform the teaching of art for decades to come. In addition adults were directed not to intervene or impose their technical and aesthetic standards upon the children's spontaneous and expressive work, soon to be known as the New Art. There was a gradual but radical change from a traditional curriculum-centred model to a more child-centred approach, which reflected the modernist values in art of expression, spontaneity and originality. Over time, curriculum content, the role and function of examinations and even the role of teachers were all questioned and, as children's artwork was left to unfold naturally, previous forms of testing or assessment were abandoned.

It is clear that Richardson did not intend this New Art to become the 'splash it all over' style that some felt it represented and indeed she was known to have encouraged the incorporation of fine calligraphic skills into the children's final compositions. Nevertheless, many teachers interpreted free expression as allowing children to create, in particular with paint, without structure, guidance or intervention; with little reference to the objective world and no reference to the work of artists for ideas or inspiration. One distinguished authority of the time is reported to have said:

> *Latterly a kind of pedagogic futurism and custom has arisen, which would have us allow children to draw unrecognisable daubs without correction, as a means of 'self expression'. We may as well encourage unintelligible and ungrammatical English with the same object. It is impossible to believe that this craze will hold the field for long, though it is obviously popular with the lazy teacher.*[4]

For some teachers, seeing their primary role more as facilitator, the provision of paints and brushes alone was seen as input enough. As a consequence, children's paintings tended to be similar in execution and outcome, as such an approach provided little opportunity for development and progression. Unsurprisingly, for many teachers and children the whole exercise lacked the creative opportunity it initially espoused and without some sort of assessment framework it proved difficult for children to progress. Anyway, how did you assess artwork, which resulted from a form of free play and experimentation, where process was more important than product and the child artist's subjective experience fundamental to the exercise?

Despite such undercurrents of concern, classroom art and craft (as it was then called), continued to promote expression, experimentation and exploration. Simpson (1987) wrote:

From these basic ideas sprang a number of concepts which carried automatic approval and which included in no particular order; imagination, interpretation, creativity, playfulness, naivety, immediacy, novelty, simplicity, imperfection and, of course the unaffected expression of feeling...corresponding to and reinforcing such notions there arose a whole set of practices, materials, techniques and a lexicon of symbols and images which together formulated and satisfied the expectations not only of teachers but also of children. The whole process was circular and self-fulfilling...[5]

The scarcity of art supplies following the war years encouraged teachers to experiment with various non-traditional art materials as substitutes. Such novel practice became of major significance in the development of primary art and design education and to some extent precipitated the gradual neglect of the comparatively modest pencil and the relatively simple act of drawing.

In 1963 an enquiry was called for into the state of primary education.[6] The committee of enquiry, chaired by Lady Plowden, produced what became known as the Plowden Report, officially entitled 'Children and their Primary Schools' and published in 1967. Based on evidence acquired from the best practices in schools at the time, the report declared its child-centred philosophy and promoted the view that within the school community children should 'live first and foremost as children and not as adults'.[7] A clear statement for the place of art in primary schools was also pronounced:

Art is both a form of communication and a means of expression of feelings, which ought to permeate the whole curriculum and the whole life of the school.[8]

The report was well received by most primary teachers, and it ignited an intense debate about the purpose and nature of compulsory education. At the same time the variety and quality of art and design education in schools began to cause concern, as a conflict was arising between those who were more intent upon teaching the content of art (art techniques, names and dates, elements and principles of design, and so on) and those who continued to see art as a means of self-expression. Children were thus either denied access to knowledge that could enhance their artwork, in the name of self-expression, or through an over emphasis on content, failed to engage in a more imaginative and intuitive approach to their work.[9]

By the 1970s public disquiet, hostile media attention and growing criticism of the predominantly child-centred and progressive education of the time became increasingly evident. The public demand was for schools to become more accountable for the curriculum they delivered, the way they delivered it and the progress and achievements of their pupils. A major review of education and educational policies, including methods of assessment was called for. In art Elliot Eisner disputed the notion of children's artistic development as a 'natural unfolding'[10] and highlighted the importance of providing children with opportunities to self-express *and* learn from instruction in art. Now the role of the adult in art education '...was seen to be in ensuring that the child's experiences were rich in stimuli and in guiding them towards models of how they might develop ways of expressing themselves'.[11] The notion of unadulterated self-expression was out.

Around this time, much was written on the importance of art and design in schools, as art educators determined to raise its status to a more central position within the curriculum. A particularly influential report commissioned by the Calouste Gulbenkian Foundation: '*The Arts in Schools – principles, practice and provision*' published in 1982[12] set out to present evidence and arguments, which would convince 'educational decision-makers at every level and in every sector...'[13] of the importance of placing the arts at the centre of the curriculum. Despite the soundness of the arguments and the persuasiveness of the case set out, the ensuing government quest for a standardized education which emphasized educational basics and redefined educational goals largely ignored much of the report. However, the need for a balanced curriculum and some sort of aesthetic education was acknowledged.[14]

The 1988 Education Reform Act not only rejected outright the child-centred educational philosophy championed by the Plowden committee and its supporters, but also the centrality of the arts as promoted by the Gulbenkian report. This paved the way for the National Curriculum with its emphasis on the core subjects of English, Mathematics and Science, complete with attainment targets and programmes of study for all children.

However, for the first time, the place of art in the school curriculum was officially secured as a foundation subject and in 1992 the National Curriculum for Art was established. The practice of drawing (sometimes termed 'recording') was revived, the investigation of materials and techniques was maintained, the use of the imagination was marginally encouraged, and for the first time in primary education the study of artists (including craftspeople and designers), artworks, art movements and styles was formally sanctioned, here termed *Knowledge and Understanding*.

The basis for assessment in art

In 1984, Keith Gentle asked in his book *Children and Art Teaching*:

> *What is the basis for our assessments and evaluations of children's art? If we never try to answer this question for ourselves much is lost to us and to our teaching.*[15]

He observed that the way in which the teacher views children's work is 'considerably different depending on whether he is examining, evaluating or assessing'.[16]

Assessment, he acknowledged, is essentially different from *Examination* and *Evaluation*: examination he described as an inappropriate form for monitoring children's progress in art and design, as it is a highly structured instrument of assessment conducted at or over a specific period of time and in relation to clearly laid down areas of learning and categories of work. Such results are then used to rate pupils according to a comparative scale of achievement.

At primary level, it has proved very difficult to specify the range of knowledge to be 'tested' in art and design. In fact, as Gentle points out, many things other than knowledge have to be considered by examiners, which depend on the examiners' experience and understanding of children's art and their capacity to interpret work presented to them. Primary school-aged children's responses to the world through their artwork, particularly their drawings, are invariably more subjective than those of adults, whilst their relatively limited experiences are no less important. Hand-eye coordination across similar age ranges naturally varies; and confidence in selecting and handling a range of materials fluctuates, often in line with the relative confidence of the teacher and according to what is required of children.

If the value of the teaching is dependent on results alone, then much of the incidental or subsidiary purpose and benefits of the art activity and the subsequent value of the children's work will be overlooked. Such contributory benefits cannot be examined as one might examine factual knowledge or a learned technique.

Evaluation, as with examination, should take place against a standard or a set of values, which will in turn determine how effective any evaluation might be. In general, Gentle believes this should take place periodically or over different lengths of time. However, in practice, whatever the task, it is impossible for the teacher not to make some sort of evaluation about how the children are responding or performing to what is asked of them. Therefore it is important that a more formal evaluation is a considered and wide ranging process, which also values the children's experience of making. Gentle believes an evaluation should evolve from a set of values, which enable the teacher to form a general or comparative view of an individual's artwork. He adds, however:

> *Both examination and evaluation say more about the strengths and failings of a course of work, than the particular educational value of any individual's experience although this is implied.*[17]

Assessment is described as a long-term view, which considers the range of a child's artwork, either in relation to previous work or the work of a particular group. The variety of work and period of time considered is important, as certain qualities may not be evident in each piece of work. The assessment might be *summative*: indicating where the child is now in terms of artistic development, or *formative*: the teacher will assess what the child or children need on the basis of what has been achieved.

The Gulbenkian report (1982) preceded the document *Art in the National Curriculum* (1992) by some ten years, yet its wide ranging and accessible doctrine provided a sound educational underpinning for art and design practices and policies in many schools. The report identified assessment as a form of educational accountability, which fulfilled an important role in keeping parents and teachers aware of the level at which the children are functioning, whilst also alerting the children to their current level of work. As in Gentle's view of evaluation, the teacher is described as making some form of informal assessment of the children's responses to an art activity all the time:

> *Assessment may take many forms, but informally teachers are assessing pupils all the time, as indeed the pupils are assessing teachers – through styles of speech, attitudes to others and to work done.*[18]

Formal assessments, in terms of grades, percentages and rank positions (e.g. examinations) are viewed as inessential, as there can 'be no statements of absolute ability'.[19] Achievements, it proposed, should be measured within the framework and context of the educational opportunity provided, as every assessment of the pupil is to some degree an assessment of the teacher and of the school.

Evaluation is presented as a review of the quality of provision and the methods employed, which look beyond the pupils to 'the style, the materials and the circumstances of the teaching and learning'.[20] Evaluation is expressed as *illuminative* and *responsive* and assessment as *pervasive* and *informative*. Illuminative evaluation goes beyond the aims and objectives of the lesson and how well these have been met. It encourages flexibility, reflection and revision of the original aims and objectives as the work progresses. Responsive evaluation is sensitive to the different types of work in terms of their 'instructional and expressive' qualities.[21] The instructional objective relates to specific skills and information to be learnt; the expressive objective is more concerned with the child's ability to explore and express ideas and feelings through the artwork itself. The two are seen as closely related, but entailing different methods of and criteria for evaluation, to which the teacher needs to be sensitive. Like Gentle (1984) the Gulbenkian report believes assessment should provide as much information as possible; however, as both evaluation and assessment involve some personal judgement based on feelings, values and intuition, most assessments we are told cannot be clinically objective.

The later, slightly different, view of art educationalist Margaret Morgan[22] sees assessment as closely related to monitoring and evaluating, with the three working together, particularly in the context of the quality of education offered to children. Morgan states that monitoring children's responses and the appropriateness of the task, takes place informally all the time. Evaluation 'is literally considering the worth, or value of the education we offer'[23] and involves looking again at our own planning and performance as teachers; looking at the understanding and performance of the children and encouraging them to look at their own approach, performance and practice. For example, where children may have responded very positively to a practical activity which involved templates and a 'Blue Peter' approach, the teacher will also need to ask how educationally worthwhile the activity was in terms of the children's creative and artistic development and progress. Practice and performance are again highlighted as integral to the assessment process. Within this framework, Morgan believes judgements are made about the qualities of the children's artwork, using a different set of criteria. These (unhelpfully) are not specified.[24]

Assessment in the National Curriculum for Art

Many teachers and art educationalists believed the document *Art in the National Curriculum* (1992) promoted the cognitive, but not the affective and intuitive modes of art and design education, and felt the issue of how to assess children's artwork continued to be a rather grey area, with much of the onus handed back to the teacher:

> *Individual pupils are required to be assessed in art at or near the end of each key stage. It is intended that assessment should be as simple and straightforward as possible and should be based on teachers' own judgements of pupils' classroom work.*[25]

Additional printed guidance upheld the intention that assessment should be simple for teachers and pupils and be on the basis of the 21 end of key stage statements[26], but also include evidence-based descriptive judgements gathered together from the teacher, pupil and teachers from an earlier stage. Teachers were also expected to keep records that tracked curriculum progress and supported the annual report to parents.

The revised *National Curriculum for Art and Design*, published in November 1999, reduced the previous two attainment targets of 'Investigating and Making' and 'Knowledge and Understanding' to one, which integrates both the theoretical and practical aspects of the subject. A new eight-level scale has also been introduced to 'clarify progression and simplify assessment' – suggesting that assessment had remained an unresolved and complex issue for teachers. Under the heading *Assessing attainment at the end of a key stage*,[27] teachers are directed to judge which of the eight level descriptors best fits the pupil's performance. Reference is then made to additional information in the QCA's annual booklets about end of key stage assessment and reporting arrangements.

The QCA (2000) publication, *Art and Design: A scheme of work for key stages 1 and 2*, provides an optional exemplar scheme of work, which can be modified for long- and medium-term planning. It is based on the National Curriculum programmes of study for art and design and shows how the subject might be taught 'to children attaining at levels broadly appropriate for their age'.[28] The document has proved to be particularly popular with schools, as it provides a government endorsed 'blueprint' for art and design practice in the primary classroom. Many schools, which may have struggled to provide a comprehensive and educationally worthwhile art programme, have appropriated the scheme of work as their art policy and content. Each unit is uniformly presented and provides a breakdown of information and points to consider under various headings. The final category is captioned *Evaluating and developing work* and provides information on learning objectives, possible teaching activities and children's learning outcomes. For example, in the unit '*What is Sculpture?*' children '*should learn*':

- *to review what they and others have done and say what they think and feel about it*
- *to identify what they might develop in their future work*[29]

Under the heading *Assessing progress* (p.15), a brief reference is made to the '*learning outcomes*' as depicted in each unit as these show '*how children might demonstrate what they have learnt*'. However, no actual reference is made to the assessment of that work in terms of a critical appraisal. Detailed records of each individual's work is not advised, as the broad descriptions of achievement provided by the end-of-unit expectations are designed to help teachers make decisions about the children's progress in relation to other children. Reasons for this difference might then be passed onto the next teacher. It is suggested, however, that a portfolio selection of the children's '*outcomes*' (note not *artwork*) from each unit be kept by the school or year group as examples of how children met the expectations.

Assessment in practice

> *Assessment in education is the process of gathering, interpreting, recording, and using information about pupil's responses to an educational task.*[30]

Art assessment largely concerns the appraisal of children's finished artwork and the process involved in making it. Although the teacher will informally assess individual pieces of work as they are produced, a fairer and more valid assessment, which also considers the child's individuality, interests and conceptual understanding, is best carried out over a period of time such as a term or a year. Individual pieces of artwork using a range of materials, media and techniques produced over time and set aside in a portfolio or folder will provide the visual information needed for the assessment. For bulkier or more sculptural work, photographs of the artwork may be included. This long-term view is important, as certain qualities in the child's work or development may not be constant and therefore not evident in each piece of work. Comparisons might also be made with previous work or in relation to the work of others so that individual progress can be monitored. Additional information can be acquired from sketchbook work as encouraged by the NC for Art and Design.

As art involves the expression of ideas and feelings, provision should also be made for opportunities to discuss the artwork with the child, so that the teacher has some insight into what the child set out to do. Assessment is probably most productive when it is shared with the child or a child is encouraged to share ideas and intentions with the rest of the class. Through observing and listening, the children's focus will be sharpened and an understanding of the many possible artistic interpretations or responses to an idea increased.

Teachers should be careful not to place too heavy an emphasis on things that can be easily measured.

> *The final outcome, the painting or pot or weaving, however attractive or eye catching, is only one measure of what the children can do or has learnt from undertaking the activity.*[31]

Qualities such as expression, imagination or inventiveness may not be easily quantified, but it is still possible to make sensitive judgements about them. For example, when looking at the visual elements of the work, such as the range of marks made in a drawing or the way the paint is employed and applied, the artwork might be described as bold, confident and expressive or light, sensitive and controlled, or there may be aspects of all or some of these. The child may have used bright, clashing colours, which create a dramatic feel to the work, or softer more subtle shades that create a calmer mood. Pattern making may be incorporated into the work, which may give a sense of rhythm and movement or simply add interesting detail to the overall aesthetic effect. The child's use of materials may be particularly inventive, suggesting not only a good imagination, but also a willingness to explore and experiment and so come up with new ways of working. Sensitive handling of the materials, may suggest a growing awareness and understanding of the characteristics and properties of particular media in different situations.

How the teacher subjectively responds to the artwork may also be of importance when making notes about or discussing it. Artwork by its very nature will engender personal responses, and it is interesting to share these in a positive way. You may also find that others share your responses. However, such notions of subjectivity must not be allowed to override the assessment, which is more about the child's learning, development and progress, and much less about the final product.

> *You are not training to be an art critic or gallery owner, but a teacher, and as such the task is to assess the learning that has taken place.*[32]

The child's ability to observe, interpret and discriminate gives some insight into perceptive skills, whilst the ability to discuss her own artwork and relate it to the work of others, using an appropriate vocabulary, indicates the growth of discursive skills. The child's attitude to art or specific art activities; the ability to follow instructions or work as part of a group or independently might also be commented on as part of the assessment.

When considering the needs of the children and in what direction to develop the artwork, the teacher's assessment may be based on the way the children work at present or how she wishes the work to progress in the future; i.e. the teacher will assess what the children need for future progress, which builds on her growing knowledge and understanding of the children's artistic abilities, alongside their range of experiences. This will include an observation of the way materials are investigated, selected, handled and manipulated; the level of individual decision-making taking place; the acquisition of skills and techniques; the formation and development of ideas and concepts and the growing knowledge and understanding of artists, art movements and the purpose and manner of art-making in different times and across the wider world.

By making collections of the children's artwork *and* making notes of discussions with children when watching children make art or review their artwork, considered assessments will be made. It may also be appropriate to allow the children to critically comment on what they have done on a child-friendly record sheet adapted to suit the age and abilities of the child, with the teacher making additional comments. Children's personal responses to their own work or perceived artistic ability is often very revealing.

Children also value the opportunity to assess their finished work, when appropriately mounted and displayed. Displays positively validate the work in a shared context and can be discussed in some depth with the children who made the work.[33]

In reality it will not be appropriate or possible to assess every piece of children's artwork. Simple records in the form of cumulative checklists will often suffice to summarize and provide data on which to base future planning or inform the next teacher. However, provision should be made for a more rigorous long-term assessment, as discussed, at meaningful intervals such as the end of a unit or scheme of work, throughout the year.

> *There is no doubt that as a teacher gains experience of talking with the children about their art, the making of assessment becomes easier and more accurate and has the effect of raising the general level of intelligence and understanding about art.*[34]

The current state of art and design assessment in primary schools

The QCA remit is to keep the curriculum under review annually and identify aspects that would benefit from further development, information and guidance. Its 2002/3 *Annual Report on Curriculum and Assessment in Art and Design*, published March 2004, stated that the expectations for children's attainment as indicated by the early learning goals for creative development and the level descriptions in Key Stages 1 and 2 of the NC for Art and Design, were considered to be reasonable by 98 per cent of the respondents for the foundation stage and 80 per cent of primary teachers. However, there was some disparity between KS1, who at 92 per cent were clearly more satisfied than the 70 per cent of KS2 respondents.

This suggests that as pupils become older, primary teachers find attainment of the level descriptions more difficult. This does not necessarily indicate that the standard of the level descriptions at KS2 are wrongly pitched, but in my view implies that a significant percentage of KS2 teachers are beginning to struggle not only with the delivery of a national curriculum in art and design, particularly given the many demands on their time, but also the assessment of it. At the foundation stage, creative development is much more central to the children's learning and there are many more creative opportunities across the curriculum. To assess children's work of this nature, in terms of its accuracy or realism is clearly inappropriate. However, it is possible to evaluate the child's ability to manipulate and experiment with materials, use of imagination and willingness to try new and different ways of working and so on, as well as respond to the finished work. Because of the greater opportunities within the foundation and KS1 curriculum for creative work with the younger children, it is likely that the teachers of this early stage are more comfortable with introducing or overseeing art-based activities, especially as in general the children will respond to such activities in a very positive and spontaneous way.

Conversely, children at KS2 often begin to express a lack of confidence in their ability to make art, and in particular drawing. For many, the ability to draw 'realistically' becomes the benchmark for measuring or assessing their own artistic ability and that of their peers, even if this is not the approach adopted by the teacher. From approximately the age of seven, children will begin to make comparisons between their work and that of others and may become frustrated or disappointed with their own achievements. The KS2 teacher may also feel inadequate in terms of artistic ability and, as a consequence, lack confidence in supporting, directing and assessing the children's artwork. As discussed earlier, this is particularly true of the primary teacher trainees with whom I work, chiefly because many abandoned art and design in the early years of their secondary education. According to Malcolm Ross,[35] in order for teacher trainees, as qualified primary teachers, to feel confident in delivering an inspiring and artistically challenging arts curriculum, they should:

a) have a clear grasp of the educational role of the arts, an understanding of how children learn through the arts, and a knowledge of the different stages of a child's development;
b) be personally interested in and familiar with at least one or two art forms;
c) be confident in encouraging creative work across the whole range of the arts;
d) **be able to recognise and evaluate the artistic quality in children's work** (my emphasis)[36]...

> *It follows that the initial training in the arts of primary school teachers, where skills can be imparted and confidence restored, is crucial. Unfortunately this training is often woefully inadequate...*[37]

Some sixteen years later there is little sign of improvement in the provision of art and design training on primary Initial Teacher Training courses. If anything the situation is worse, as the already inadequate amount of time provided for the teaching of art and design has been repeatedly cut, to make way for the increased emphasis on core subjects and extended teaching experiences in school. However, according to the QCA Report (2004), it appears that the QCA/DfES schemes of work for Key Stages 1 and 2 are providing good support for teachers' planning, particularly in the areas of improving progression within a unit and continuity over a key stage:

> *Teachers using these units were clearer about what children should learn and the resources needed to meet their objectives.*[38]

On the other hand it was noted teachers still 'need a clear understanding of art and design objectives and other subject objectives if art and design is not to be used as a service to others.'[39]

An end of unit assessment, informal interim individual or group assessment, target setting and review, marking of homework, formal self-assessments by pupils and individual interaction between teacher and pupil were identified as the key components of a meaningful assessment programme. Within this framework, however, recent Ofsted evaluations had found that assessment of pupil performance and the use of such assessment for short-term planning of lessons and activities were inadequate in just under a quarter of primary schools. In over a third of schools, procedures for assessing pupils' performance over time and to guide curriculum planning were also weak. Target setting in art and design was used by only a few.[40]

Many secondary schools it observed received 'little or no information from primary schools on pupils' capability in art and design',[41] intimating that assessment of children's art and design work in the primary school is either neglected or any assessment that takes place is for in-house purposes only. Secondary teachers have thus relied on transition days, when year 6 pupils from feeder schools spend time in the art department, or from inter-phase arts events to gain insight into pupil performance. Of those secondary schools that did receive information from primary schools about the pupils' performance, 44 per cent of art and design departments found the level descriptions very useful or quite useful, whilst 55 per cent found them not very useful or of no use at all. In the closing pages of the report, two recommendations for the future QCA team were:

- *look at strategies for developing critical discrimination and the ability to make aesthetic judgements in art and design*
- *develop further examples for art and design, on line, of pupils' work at different levels of attainment, with commentaries that support formative and summative assessment.*[42]

Such recommendations appear to be in line with the thinking evident in the Gulbenkian report (1982) and the writing of Gentle (1984).

To conclude, the QCA report (2004) provides some insight into the current state of play with regard to the assessment of art and design in many primary schools. Although limited in its remit, the report's findings suggest, as I originally commented, that good quality assessment of children's art and design work continues to be a problematic issue, which is not easily addressed. Without adequate experience in the making of art and design at school (or elsewhere) and comprehensive training and experience in the teaching of art and design on ITT courses, many teachers will continue to lack the confidence and expertise required to provide a worthwhile art education for primary school children, which they feel qualified to assess from an informed perspective. A positive and varied experience of art and design coupled with a sound knowledge base will enable the primary teacher to lead, support and direct an educationally enriching, meaningful and developmentally fitting art programme for children, which will also provide the criteria for assessment. As David Best, author of *Feeling and Reason in the Arts*, stated: 'Good art must provide the criteria for tests, not the tests provide the criteria for good art'.[43] Recent government initiatives to promote creativity[44] must go hand in hand with further investment in art and design courses for both primary trainees and teachers if effective progress is to be made in the delivery and assessment of art and design in primary schools in the future.

Notes and references

1. *Art and design: The National Curriculum for England Key Stages 1-3* (1999), Jointly published by the Department for Education and Qualifications and Curriculum Authority.
2. *Art and design: A scheme of work for key stages 1 and 2* (2000), Qualifications and Curriculum Authority.
3. The artist Franz Cizek held art classes in Vienna, for children aged approximately 4–14 years at the beginning of the twentieth century. The work received great public approval and Cizek became known as the father of *Child Art*. The children's work was introduced to a number of countries, including Britain, as a touring exhibition.
4. Carline, R (1968), *Draw they must*, Edward Arnold, p. 13.
5. Simpson, A (1987), *What is Art Education Doing?* Journal of Art and Design Education, vol. 6, no. 3, p. 254.
6. The Secretary of State for Education, Sir Edward Boyle.
7. The Plowden Report (1967), *Children and their Primary Schools*, CACE, paragraph 505.
8. *Ibid.*, paragraph 676.
9. Efland, A D (1990), *A History of Art Education*, Teachers College Press, p. 263.
10. Anning, A & Ring, K (2004), *Making Sense of Children's Drawings*, Open University Press.
11. *Ibid.*
12. Robinson, K (ed.) (1982), *The Arts in Schools: Principles, practice and provision*, Calouste Gulbenkian Foundation, p.21.
13. Aspin, D N (1984), *Objectivity and Assessment in the Arts: The Problem of Aesthetic Education*, paper delivered at the University of London, Institute of Education to the National Association for Education in the Arts (27th April).
14. Sir Keith Joseph (1984) in his speech to the North of England Education Conference in Sheffield.
15. Gentle, K (1984), *Children and Art Teaching 5-13 series*, Croom Helm, p.185.
16. *Ibid.*
17. *Ibid.*, p.188.
18. Robinson, K *op. cit.*, p. 82.
19. *Ibid.*
20. *Ibid.*
21. Robinson, K *op. cit.*, p. 83.
22. Morgan, M (ed.) (1988), ART *4-11 Art in the early years of schooling*, Blackwell.
23. *Ibid.*, p. 120.

24. *Ibid.*
25. *Art in the National Curriculum (England)* (1992), Department of Education and Science, HMSO, p. 4.
26. *Art in the National Curriculum (England) op. cit.*, section E, 1.1 and 1.2.
27. *Art and Design The National Curriculum for England*, *op. cit.*, p. 38.
28. *Art and design: a scheme of work for key stages 1 and 2* Teachers'guide (2000), QCA, p. 3.
29. *Art and design: a scheme of work for key stages 1 and 2*, QCA, Unit 1C: What is Sculpture?
30. Pollard, A (1996), *Reflective Teaching in the Primary School*, Cassell.
31. Penny, Ford, Price and Young (2002), *Achieving QTS, Teaching Arts in Primary Schools*, Learning Matters Ltd, p. 48.
32. *Ibid.*
33. Callaway, G & Kear, M (1999), *Teaching Art and Design in the Primary School*, David Fulton Publishers, p. 13.
34. Gentle, K *op. cit.*, p. 192.
35. Ross, M (1989), *The Arts in the Primary School: Reforming Teacher Education*, Calouste Gulbenkian Foundation.
36. *Ibid.*, p. 3.
37. *Ibid.*, p. 4.
38. *Art and design: A scheme of work for key stages 1 and 2*, QCA, *op. cit.*, 4.1, p. 19.
39. *Ibid.*
40. *Ibid.*
41. *Ibid.*
42. *Ibid.*
43. David Best [author of *Feeling and Reason in the Arts* (1985) Allen and Unwin] keynote address at North of England conference: *New Perspectives in the Arts*, April 1989.
44. See *Primary National Strategy Excellence and Enjoyment: learning and teaching in the primary years* (2004), DfES.

Chapter 3: The assessment of GCSE Art: Criterion-referencing and cognitive abilities

Trevor Rayment and Brian Britton

Concepts of *art* and *assessment* are mutually and implacably hostile. Assessment seeks to objectify and define, and when applied to art, it tends to regulate and constrain an activity which is essentially autonomous and open-ended. But the everyday practice of evaluating art continues regardless of such objections, and our normal relationships with art are most commonly expressed in terms of evaluation: appreciating art, valuing it, liking or disliking it. That we can talk about art at all is confirmation of our readiness to evaluate it, and the language used is often the implicit language of assessment: what's taught in that lesson is art; she is good at art; Picasso was the greatest twentieth-century artist, and so on. However, this mode of talk, which historically has typified also the language of evaluation in art education, may not support the unconditional model of objective analysis which is now required to maintain the status of the subject in an increasingly competitive curriculum, and the relative value of its qualifications in the world beyond school. In our post-Ofsted, post-National Curriculum education system the universal watchword is 'accountability', and assessment in art must be demonstrably as transparent, reliable and representative as assessment in any other area of activity.

At secondary school level, over the last decade or more, the most conspicuous response to these demands has been the introduction of criterion-referenced assessment. A primary appeal to the assessment of achievement in art based on subjective qualities of intuition, feeling or expression has been displaced by the assessment of attainment measured under a matrix of explicit assessment objectives and marking criteria. Thus, from 1995 until 2002, success in GCSE Art required, in any body of work presented for assessment, clear evidence of these six stated objectives:[1]

- Record responses to direct experience, observation and imagination
- Develop ideas for their work, investigating visual and other sources of information
- Explore and use a range of media for working in two and/or three dimensions
- Review, modify and refine work as it progresses and realise intentions
- Identify the distinctive characteristics of art, craft and design and relate them to the context in which the work was created, making connections with their own work
- Make critical judgements about art, craft and design, using a specialist vocabulary

A case has been robustly made[2] that the above assessment criteria have been responsible for a wholly undesirable orthodoxy of course content and student response. However, the question for this paper is not about the value or validity of these procedures, or whether the criteria are inappropriate to any particular analysis of art, but whether there is any evidence to be had about the objectivity, accuracy or reliability, in whatever ways these can be demonstrated, of criterion-based assessment for GCSE Art, and its objects or intentions, as expressed in those criteria. It was anticipated that it may be possible to discover such evidence, if it existed, by comparing assessment data from GCSE Art to data obtained from an established formal measure of cognitive ability.

The sample for this enquiry was drawn from a large mixed, 11-18 comprehensive school in the south of England. Full access was provided to moderated GCSE Art marks for all candidates from that school (412 in total), for the years 1996 to 2002 inclusive. This represents the entire period of the application of the six assessment objectives listed above. Revised objectives were introduced for the syllabus for first examination in 2003 (now re-designated *Art and Design*). During the period covered by the analysis the AQA GCSE Art syllabus was followed in that school, and all work submitted for examination was marked according to the six assessment criteria listed above. Year 9 NFER-Nelson Cognitive Abilities Test (CAT) scores (Verbal, Quantitative and Non-verbal Batteries) for all GCSE Art candidates were also provided by the school to the enquiry. The tests are claimed to be an effective predictor of future academic achievement. The NVR (Non-verbal Reasoning) test may provide the best indication of 'general intelligence' as it measures the ability to reason without the need to draw on learned knowledge. The other two tests are dependent to a greater degree on the subject's acquired knowledge and skills. An Internet search revealed that the tests are widely used in UK schools as a predictor of likely success in GCSE, frequently for 'value-added' purposes: for example, to support the assessment of teachers' salary threshold applications.

It was anticipated then that it may be possible to draw some conclusions about the reliability of the GCSE assessment by directly comparing data from the examination with CAT scores of those same pupils. The CAT scores are norm-referenced and are presented here in an age-related form. On the charts below this is referred to as SAS (the Standard Age Score) and is recorded on a scale in which the mean score for each age group is set at 100 and the standard deviation at 15. These provide no information about performance relative to any scale of fixed values but show each candidate's standing relative to others in that age group, calculated on a national basis. NFER-Nelson publish[3] their own analysis of the association between GCSE Art and Design grades and CAT scores. This is expressed in terms of a prediction of the probability of achieving any particular grade by students achieving a specific CAT score. For example, it is claimed that a student with a CAT score of <70 has a 0 per cent probability of achieving grade A, whilst for a student scoring >130 the probability of achieving grade A is 49 per cent.

The data employed in this study are then of fundamentally different kinds. This must be taken into consideration in any discussion of a potential relationship between them. GCSE marks are of course criterion-referenced. They are not age related and claim to measure performance objectively over a range of practical and critical aesthetic or artistic dimensions against those criteria defined by the six assessment objectives outlined above. GCSE Art comprises two assessed components: coursework and controlled test. The marks were awarded in the range 0–24 for each component and, as represented in this paper, are as moderated by the Examination Board's agreed procedures and provided to schools after the publication of results. Marks for individual candidates are scaled by the Board to achieve the 60 per cent coursework and 40 per cent controlled test weighting specified in the Regulations.[4] The scaled and combined marks are translated into the grades A*-G which are finally awarded to students.

The box plot graphs below were chosen as a means of providing a graphic illustration of emerging relationships between the two sets of data. The box plot is able to show quite complex information in a reasonably accessible graphical form. The line across the box represents the median value. The box contains the central 50 per cent of cases, and the 'whiskers' extend to the largest and smallest values that are not classified as outliers. In these graphs an outlier is defined as a value which is more than 1.5 box-lengths from the box itself. These are shown on the graph as **o**, with the appropriate case number. In the graphs below, each box represents those students who have been awarded a specific mark, for coursework (CWK) or controlled test (PA/Practical Assignment). Both the mark band and the number of students from the total sample achieving that mark are defined on the category axis. This can be compared directly with CAT scores by reading across to the vertical axis.

Although each separate mark band represents a wide range of CAT scores, and on a first reading there appears to be considerable overlap between the upper and lower quartiles of adjacent box plots (i.e. of adjacent marks), closer examination of the original data shows that this overlap may be somewhat less significant than it appears. It was noted, for example (*Chart (iv)*), that although CAT NVR scores for the lower quartile of the group who achieved a controlled test (PA) mark of 17 extended from 83 to 100, eleven of the twelve scores were in the range 89 to 100. Again, whilst the lower quartile of the 21 (PA) mark band scored between 83 and 103 on CAT NVR, five of these six scores were in the range 94 to 103.

There are several other anomalies which, from a first reading of the charts, seem to upset an otherwise fairly predictable relationship between GCSE marks and CAT scores: for example, NVR scores for those who achieved the GCSE PA mark 6 (*Chart (iv)*) seem relatively high, but here it should be noted that the box represents only two students. Their poor performance in the controlled test was readily explained by teaching staff, as was the lowest coursework mark 8, achieved by a student with high CAT scores in each battery. All other untypical values were analysed in this way, and in most cases staff were able to offer reasons (attitude, application or personal circumstances) for the more obvious differences between GCSE marks achieved and the level of performance that those pupils' measured cognitive abilities might otherwise seem to predict. It would not be appropriate to discuss all the exceptional cases here.

Examination of the charts also reveals a somewhat arbitrary relationship between CAT/SAS scores and the controlled test (PA) box plots representing marks below 12. In contrast the coursework charts seem to show a more consistent and progressive association in the lower mark bands. It is noted however that the coursework marks are higher overall in the lower bands, indeed, only two students from the entire population were awarded below 10 marks. There is a readily available explanation for this effect: teachers have an absolute commitment to students' examination success and here have been able to ensure that all candidates produce coursework, and evidence of all assessment objectives, to at least a minimum prescribed level. Whilst the controlled test is closely supervised, it is essentially unaided, and teachers are unable to influence the quality of work produced to the same degree. In the lower mark bands work shows less evidence of the assessment criteria, and the failure by students to provide any evidence towards one or more criteria, as often happens, may have caused the irregularity seen here.

Does this analysis reveal anything of value about GCSE assessment? Certainly there is a demonstrable association between the measure of attainment in GCSE Art and these other claimed representations of intelligence. But this may be no more than common sense would have us predict, even without the evidence of an empirical comparison, for most human activity is in one way or another a function of cognitive ability. And whilst there may be various reasons to expect a more explicit association in respect of non-verbal reasoning (reflecting innate ability), or verbal reasoning (reflecting social, cultural or educational factors), examination of the charts suggests that the association would seem to be strongest and most clearly defined in respect of the quantitative battery. That seems somewhat contradictory under an expressive, intuitive, free-ranging vision of art education, but perhaps does make some sense in terms of the reductionist, prescriptive exercise that, many would assert, assessment in school-based art has become.

The situation may be worse yet, for the assessment criteria are not simply applied to the processes and products of open-ended and justfiable learning activities in art. There is considerable pressure on teachers to 'teach to' the criteria. Indeed, it is common practice to display the objectives on classroom walls to remind pupils of the need to demonstrate explicitly adherence to these requirements in their coursework and controlled test submissions. Thus the criteria dominate every stage of 'art' making, from conception to production. This begs fundamental questions about the nature and purposes of art education, about the acceptability of predicting outcomes in this way, and about the position of the subject in schools relative to a wider definition of art. On the other hand, there are also questions to be answered about maintaining the status of art relative to other subjects on the curriculum and about the role of assessment in monitoring the quality of teaching and learning processes.[5]

However, it is not the purpose of this enquiry to question whether the GCSE criteria represent a sufficient, legitimate or appropriate account of students' achievement in art. Certainly the GCSE marks studied do seem to represent a measure of attainment that has some form of overall symmetry with what their CAT scores suggest we might otherwise expect of those students. It would seem reasonable therefore to make a tentative claim, based on the comparisons of this paper, about the 'reliability' of this indicator, within its limited terms of reference. The pedagogical, philosophical or moral justification of criterion-referenced assessment in school-based art remains a matter for further debate.

Originally published in *The International Journal of Art & Design Education* 23. 2, 2004.

Notes and references

1. SCAA/ACAC, (1995), GCSE Regulations and Criteria, p.21.
2. Binch, N, Robertson, L (1994), *Resourcing and Assessing Art, Craft and Design*, NSEAD, Corsham.
3. http://www.nfer-nelson.co.uk
4. SCAA/ACAC *(Ibid.)*
5. For a thorough examination of these and related issues, see Boughton, D, Eisner, E W, Ligtvoet, J (eds) (1996), *Evaluating and Assessing the Visual Arts in Education*, Teachers College Press, New York.

Chart (i)

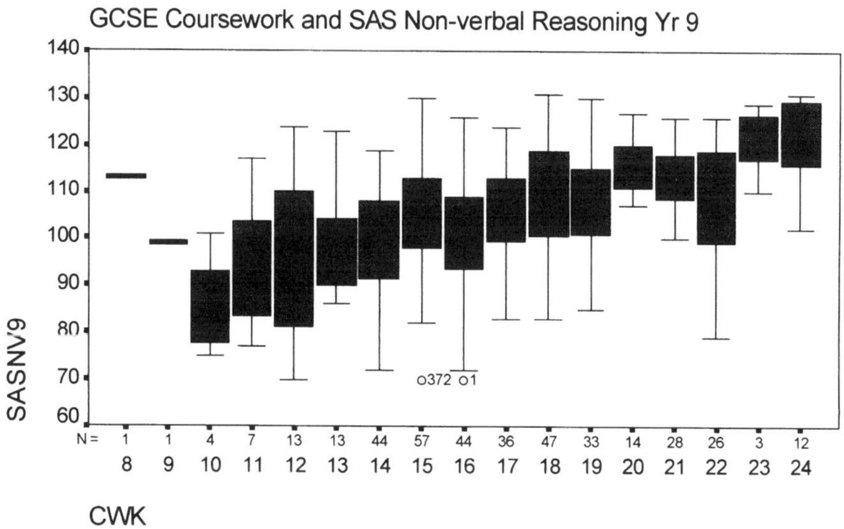

Chart (ii)

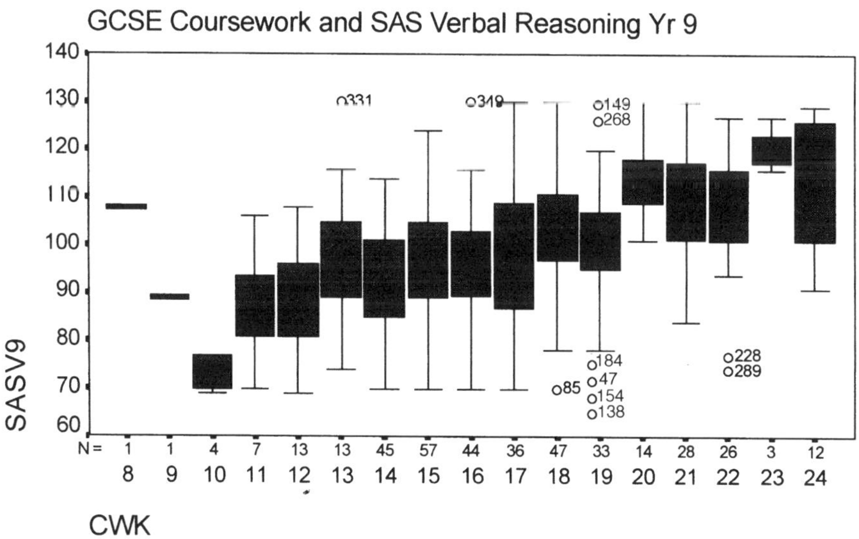

Chart (iii)

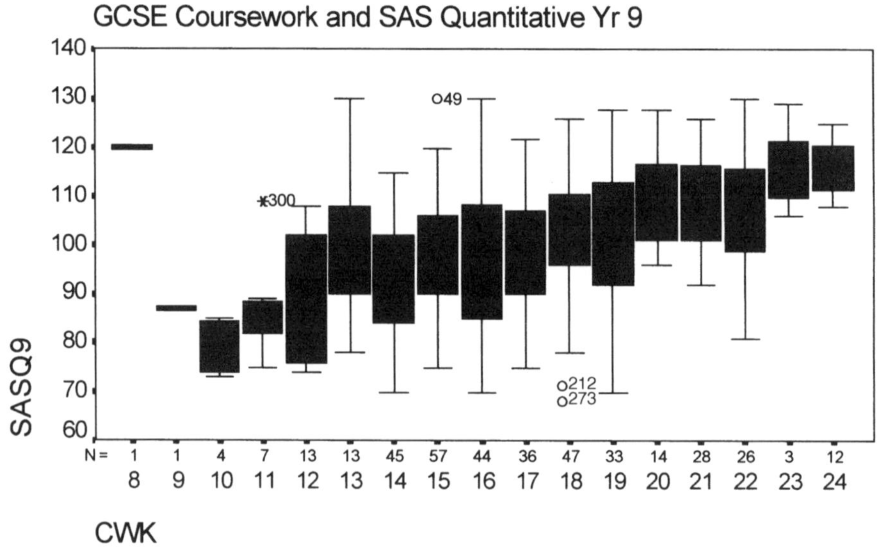

Chart (iv)

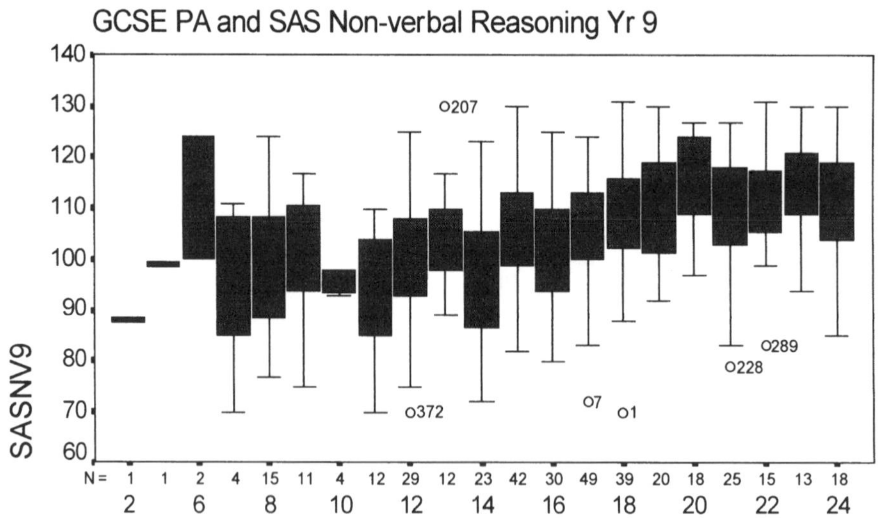

Chart (v)

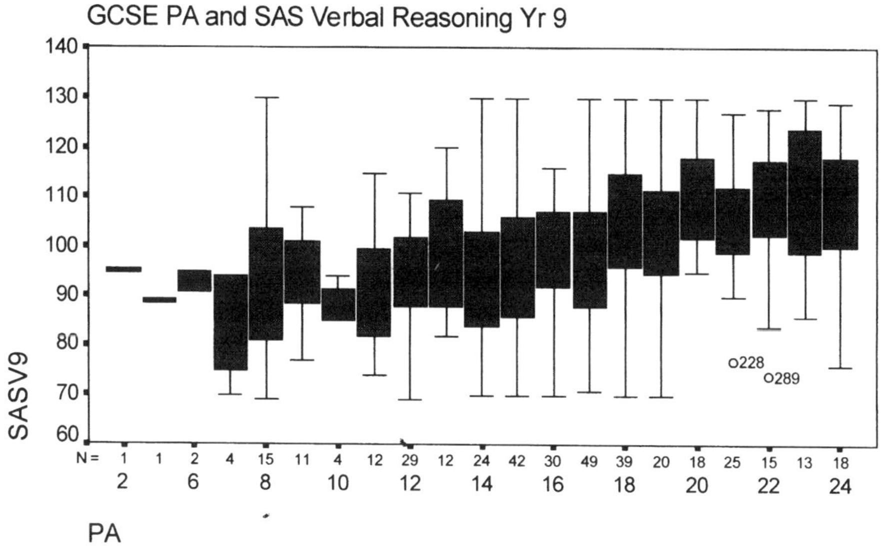

Chart (vi)

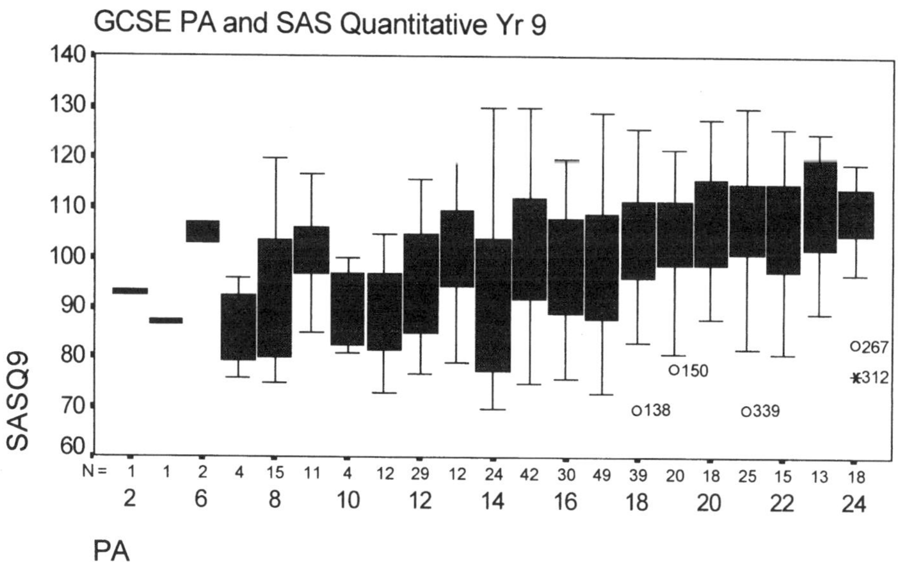

Chapter 4: AS Level Art: Farewell to the 'Wow' factor?

Tom Hardy

Overview

The AS level modular exams for year 12 students were introduced as part of the government's Curriculum 2000 reforms and were designed to bring greater breadth to the year 12 and 13 experience.

A uniform structure of two modules, followed by a synoptic timed test, has been imposed on all subjects by the Qualifications and Curriculum Authority [QCA]. In AS level art the Expressive Study module requires evidence of a broad engagement with different generic art forms and visual language skills; the Thematic Study requires convergence towards specific outcomes in at least two media; and the timed test of eight hours duration requires work towards a single theme with a preparatory period of six weeks. The paper for the examined module arrives in February, so the two coursework modules need to be completed in a little more than a term.

The four assessment objectives are as follows:

- To record observations, experiences, ideas, information and insights in visual and other forms, appropriate to intentions.
- To analyse, and evaluate critically, sources such as images, objects, artefacts and texts, showing understanding of purposes, meanings and contexts.
- To develop ideas through sustained investigation and exploration, selecting and using materials, processes and resources, identifying and interpreting relationships and analysing methods and outcomes.
- To present a personal, coherent and informed response, realizing intentions and articulating and explaining connections with the work of others.

All four objectives need to be met in each module.

Although some subjects have welcomed the change, it seems that fears raised by those concerned with the teaching of art during the consultation process have been born out by the experience of subsequent years.

Under the previous system, art teachers were free to address skills and concepts in their own way and with regard to the different aptitudes, interests and learning styles of their students. The final submission, including the exam project was marked as a whole, relying on the experience of the teacher and moderators to balance the requirements of the syllabus with the transcendent, the 'wow factor'.

This paper questions the value of a modular and assessment objective-led course that is at once superficial in its expectations, draconian in content, unrealistic in its timescale and discouraging of work of substance.

AS LEVEL ART: Farewell to the 'Wow' factor?

> *Understanding Poetry... if a poem's score for perfection is plotted on the horizontal of a graph and its importance is plotted on the vertical, then calculating the total area of the poem yields its greatness.*

Oh, how we laughed at this pastiche of a bygone age in the film *Dead Poets Society* as the philistine reductionists were lampooned by Robin Williams's personification of enlightened teaching, Mr Keating. How many of us, after seeing that film, stored away the phrase 'carpe diem' as a touchstone of our own (hoped for) shamanistic practice?

Well, we're not laughing now as, trapped in the ultimate spiral curriculum, we seem forever doomed to revisit the mistakes of that unenlightened and unlamented past.

Having refined, polished and set a shining gem of a course over the previous ten years, and presided over a period where standards rose inexorably and without parallel in other subject areas, our accomplishment is now to be consigned to a file marked 'too good to be true'. Its replacement, a series of bite-size chunks with a lowest common denominator of expectation and where continuity and sustained investigation are positively discouraged. To paraphrase Keating in the film, 'We're not laying pipe here', we are talking about art!

I must admit that when the course was first mooted, I felt a degree of excitement at the prospect of built-in deadlines which would finally give weight to our competition for students' time when modular exams in other subject areas bottleneck throughout the year, and a simple structure to fall back on, occasionally to allow the 'teacher as shaman' a day off. Indeed, I left the first meetings with Edexcel (rather worryingly entitled 'Looking Back and Moving Forward') feeling that much had been done to retain the flexibility required for exciting and effective teaching. However, as the precursory year progressed, the tone of those presenting each successive meeting became more and more exasperated as the QCA blocked elements of good practice, presumably on the assumption that they were merely the shibboleths of a vested interest group. When those employed to fire our enthusiasm used such phrases as 'There is no logic to it...', 'Students are guinea pigs in a horrible experiment...' and 'I am not allowed to say what I really think of this...', one knew that things were rapidly going pear-shaped. My fears were confirmed when I saw extracts from the induction video. Although peppered with talk of 'building on good practice', prescription and prohibition had resulted in exemplar material from pilot schools that was so dull and devoid of wit it took my breath away. My idea of a good sketchbook is of an open-ended tool for research and exploration; evidence of an individual path of discovery, not the series of formulaic and dedicated exercises exemplified therein. I wonder how many examiners thought they would scream if they saw another colour wheel.

Of course, true to the shambles of the whole exercise the complete video was not delivered until after the exam paper had been distributed in February!

Structure

The six unit structure applies to all the new GCE specifications. The advantage of a common structure across the subjects was felt to outweigh the disadvantages.[1]

With that glib statement from Rob Taylor of the QCA, concerns from art teachers about such a structure were brushed aside during a travesty of a consultation period. Bureaucratic convenience took precedence over decades of published research on the dangers of a framework which inevitably results in 'teaching to the test'.

Art, from any modern perspective, is an open-ended activity with outcomes which are the result of individual and personal programmes of study within the bounds of the student's 'cognitive map'. Indeed, Victor Pasmore, with his educationalist's hat on, said, in 1959, that 'a modern course should assume a relative outlook in which only the beginning is defined and not the end'[2] and more recently Nicolas Serota, Director of Tate Modern, encapsulated the postmodern mindset when he remarked, 'There will not always be an answer to every question. Art obliges us to answer questions for ourselves'.[3]

Ideally this deconstructionist ethos should have knock-on benefits for all areas of the curriculum in terms of the development of inquiry and independent research. These are the key skills, eminently transferable, that should be sought from the arts and these are the skills which have been most fundamentally marginalized by the changes.

Maurice Barrett warned in his book *Art Education: a strategy for course design* that we need to 'avoid formulae and strategies which others, from different disciplines, insist that we adopt so that they can achieve 'a unified standard'.[4] This was echoed in the NSEAD's response to the consultation document on subject criteria in which John Steers stated that 'a modular structure has few advantages in Art and Design and is likely to lead to fragmentation of the subject and increase orthodoxy of approach'.[5]

In ignoring what makes art different, the philistines overlook the subject's importance as a necessarily divergent foil to the convergent curricular core. Art students need elbow room for the pursuit of a personal aesthetic and a modular straitjacket does them no favours at all. Certainly, I have watched my brightest students struggle to reconcile their desire to produce idiosyncratic work of substance with the need to jump through the circumscribed hoops necessary for the all-important grades. Risky experimentation and open-ended exploration have been reduced to a minimum and it seems as though the course has been deliberately designed to reward mediocrity. That joy at seeing students transcend the shackles of the syllabus becomes an increasing rarity as the built-in ceilings of the new course result in work that is merely the sum of its many parts.

Time

It seemed like a race. I used to go to galleries out of enjoyment but this year I kept thinking that I was wasting my time if an exhibition was not relevant to a particular project.[6]

To pursue the open-ended briefs, which are peculiar to all the arts, requires time to think, to ruminate and to consolidate skills appropriate to the task. This overloaded course allows for very little thinking time. The situation is exacerbated by the hermetically sealed nature of the three separate units (six including those at A2) and the requirement to re-prove skills in each dedicated work journal rather than to progress with, and develop, personal themes. If, for instance, a drawing of a skeleton is equally appropriate as preparation towards a figure project as it is for a unit on natural forms, it must be duplicated rather than serve both. Furthermore, in an incomprehensible change to the original specifications, we were told that we could not re-submit AS material as developmental prep for units at A2. Finished work in year 13 is therefore not seen in the context of its development unless time is spent replicating it.

There is also an imbalance of workload between the two years. The requirement to submit two projects with finished work in at least four media as AS coursework seems heavy-handed compared with a short essay and a practical coursework unit which requires no conclusion at all at A2, especially as a year 13 student, with a reduction in subjects, will have a much more generous timetable allocation.

Standards

It is sobering that, during the introductory year, for the first time in many years, students of mine returned from university open days glum with the impression that the new art exams would no longer count as academic qualifications. Indeed, one admissions tutor questioned the value of AS level qualifications in general claiming that they 'militate against academic excellence'. This is a great shame. Through the rigorous critical study element of the old syllabus it seemed, finally, that the argument was ours. This hard-won reputation, however, has been seriously dented. The contextual study has been reduced to a cursory 2000 words and is to be set at A2, once the bulk of the practical work has been completed, thus rendering it meaningless as an inductive exercise. If the pilot projects are to be our exemplars, the bulk of the written requirement over two years now rests with rather prosaic descriptions of processes and even these are subject to penalties which I believe have no place in a field which values iconoclasm. Where will a student stand, I wonder, whose personal creative manipulation of language (Internet-inspired lower case, esoteric use of punctuation etc.) falls entirely within the remit of art but outside that of English?

With the imposition of two short, timed tests set to lazy one word exam 'papers', reminiscent of the CSE of old, I feel that it is also time that art teachers questioned the value of timed tests of any duration which, in this postmodern age, seem singularly inappropriate for art. I recall that during meetings in the early 1990s when the London Board, as was, last changed its syllabus, the timed element, even then, was regarded as archaic but a workable twenty hours was retained for pragmatic reasons to give art teachers leverage with school managers to suspend the timetable for art practicals. With the time allowance reduced to a derisory eight hours (and twelve for A2) we are in danger of eradicating work of ambition and scale. I would argue that pace has nothing to say about a student's ability in this subject. Again, representatives of examining boards have been apologetic about this imposition and have suggested a strategy whereby it is an element of prep that is timed. I suggest that no valid information can be gained about a student's research with this artificial showcasing; indeed valid priorities are inevitably skewed.

We were told that, as regards expected standards, the exam would 'find its own level' following an analysis of the first year's submission. This was disingenuous of the government. This meant that teachers, flying blind, had to squeeze blood from hard-pressed students in order to ensure grades in a year without reference to prior exemplar material. The standard was artificially high, as, in teaching to stay ahead of pack, we inadvertently became the pack, and, in doing so, inflated grade expectations and made a rod for our own backs. I had the opportunity to question Andrew Adonis (education adviser in Blair's kitchen cabinet) about this, naively thinking that a view from the ground might usefully inform policy. In a moment of surprising candour he revealed that this had always been part of the government's plan to 'raise standards'. He went on to intimate that overloaded courses were considered essential to keep students on the ball, and that the whole concept of independent study periods was anathema to the New Labour work ethic. David Blunkett, of course, went on to reinforce this view in the press with his defensive suggestion that, in previous years, the lower sixth was little more than an extension of the summer holiday. One is reminded of the cavalier attitude displayed by Duncan Graham, the first chairman of the NCC, at the time of the imposition of a similarly overloaded national curriculum, who wrote that it 'was better to over-prescribe and then draw back than to under-prescribe and try to tighten up'.[7] This would seem to be a policy constant.

Assessment

It is all about proof and documentation rather than the finished product.[8]

All attempts [to reduce] art to component parts seek by implication to avoid the essence of artistic or aesthetic discovery.[9]

In 1991 the NSEAD response to the Interim report of the National Curriculum art working group warned of 'valuing only those aspects of subjects which can be readily measured'.[10] Such constraints were recognized and tackled at classroom level and the efforts of teachers not only prevented the mechanistic nightmare envisaged on paper but absorbed, circumnavigated and improved upon the brief while retrieving ownership of the process. Such imaginative and subversive finessing is required again as we find ourselves immersed in a 'reducto ad absurdum' assessment procedure which lacks continuity and coherence at all levels. In the language of the new taxonomy, the hierarchy of descriptors places 'fluency' above 'confidence' at both GCSE and A2 level. At AS level, expectations do not rise above 'confident'. Personally I have higher expectations of my students.

This lack of coherence was vividly illustrated at one trial marking session during which we looked at two sample portfolios. One contained precocious work which could have been taken for that of a degree student, and the other, very mediocre work of sub-GCSE standard. Without a hint of irony, it was demonstrated that the latter should be rewarded the higher mark as, unaware of his shortcomings, he had 'confidently' completed a project which displayed little sophistication. Regardless of work that involved an idiosyncratic pursuit of ideas, problem solving and the refining of technique, the former was downgraded because of a written commentary deemed to be insufficient. In spite of the original draft specifications which stated that 'shortcomings in some aspects of the examination may be balanced by better performance in others', it is clear that the equal weighting for all objectives has inevitably led to the rewarding of the spurious over the essential.

Elliot Eisner wrote in 1973:

> *Critics of art, literature, music, dance and poetry do not assign painters, writers, composers dancers and poets behavioural objectives. Yet critics lose no time in evaluating their work. One does not have to have an objective in order to evaluate or appraise the quality of experience or of art. One can and does look backwards, as it were, not to see if artists realised specific objectives that were assigned in advance but rather to determine what they did achieve. Indeed art at its best enables both critics and artists to expand their criteria regarding the nature and quality of art. Some of the greatest art forms man has produced have been iconoclastic. They fit none of the criteria that existed at the time they were created.*[11]

With an awareness of this equal weighting, my guinea pig cohort of students spent precious time, which could have been spent running with a theme, returning again and again to dot 'i's and cross 't's. This headlong rush through content, at the expense of independent analysis, reflection and the kind of chance discovery that leads to exciting and exceptional work, led one of my students to comment after the exam was over that she didn't feel that she had moved on from GCSE.

This is a worry which has been flagged by Dr Ann Hodgson of the Institute of Education in an evaluation of the new courses. Her concern is that teachers will also forgo exciting and risk-taking teaching in order to 'teach to the test'.[12] The corollary of an increasingly didactic approach will, of course, be a widening gulf between school study skills and expectations at college level.

> *At its most successful, art, more than any other subjects, presents the possibility of a complete synthesis of experience.*[13]

Since Dewey's research of the early twentieth century, it has been acknowledged by most that children are holistic learners and, over the past ten years particularly, art teachers have refined and developed, at sixth form level, a model of holistic and open-ended learning. In spite of mission statements to the contrary, curriculum planners seem determined to hark back to an age when art was a series of short technical experiments with predetermined outcomes, seemingly convinced that, with a little push, art and science would eventually reconcile. I would argue that art has always had much more in common with philosophy. Indeed, through Socratic dialogue rather than spoon-feeding, the intellectual engagement with the subject today is profoundly removed from the skills-led syllabus of old. Hand in hand with a holistic regard for the individual student came a holistic approach to assessment. This was, of course, problematic at first with those of the convergent school, the 'tick box jury'. However, through dedicated analysis and refinement over the years, moderation and what the Americans refer to as the gestalt factor (the artist and teacher Allan Kaprow called it the 'wow'[14] effect), what resulted was an accurate method for judging rigour without compromising the individual nature of each submission. I would suggest that a marking scheme of eight separate targets, each with a maximum of eight marks, as well as being stultifyingly tedious, is less reliable. It is a natural inclination of arts teachers not to award marks which imply perfection. We tend towards what Martha Graham described as 'Divine Dissatisfaction',[15] the creative impulse that things could always be better (ring a bell, Mr

Blair?). This impulse has little detrimental effect on grades when marking to a percentage but when eight is the maximum available score in eight separate boxes, the tendency upon aggregation will undoubtedly be to drag grades down.

This lack of trust of teachers and students alike to keep their noses to the grindstone is most pointedly illustrated by the QCA's extraordinary belt and braces approach to assessment. If all units are to be examined, why the synoptic requirement for the timed test which, once again, requires students to backtrack and showcase skills already in evidence?

It is also apparent that comparing those who enter modular units in year 12 with those who enter all units in year 13 is unfair to the former. Year 13 students are able to top up units with work displaying their most recent skill levels and have more time to edit and refine. Students, whose learning curves are shallow to begin with, are thus penalized under the modular structure. Much as I wish that all my students were tortoises rather than hares, the requirement to time manage effectively and work with consistency in year 12 in order to ensure an A grade at A2 is unrealistic and ignores the more usual, and more natural, pattern of learning. In the spring 2000 edition of Education Research, Billy McClune of the Graduate School of Education of Queen's University Belfast found, presumably without too much expenditure of grey matter, that 'Upper 6th students performed better than an equivalent group of pupils in the lower 6th year when tested with the same examination'. His findings went on to show clearly that in 'a modular system which allows pupils to go through the assessment process at different stages, pupils opting for modular assessment midway through the course may be at a disadvantage compared with those who opt for assessment at the end of the course'.

This confusion over standards, and the inequity of the dual modular/ linear assessment 'playing field' is compounded with the insidious return of the process that dare not speak its name – norm referencing. Why will no one talk openly about the return of this monster? Examiners speak of it in hushed tones. They make it clear that it is a taboo topic of conversation while referring to it by a number of aliases, but, whatever weasel words are used, an ever shifting grade boundary (always upwards in art) indicates statistical manipulation and, given the absolute denial from ministers of its existence, a hidden political agenda. A few years ago, the Chief Examiner, the late Bill Reid, was more forthcoming. He warned that the government was sensitive to the perennial press reports suggesting that exams were getting easier and that anything above a 2 per cent hike in higher grades in the coming year would activate a norm referenced change in boundaries. Yet, when this did indeed occur and it was questioned, Malcolm Wicks, then Under Secretary of State for Education, stated that it is:

> *...wrong to suggest that there has been a return to norm referenced grading or predetermined success-rates at GCSE and A level. Students who meet the established standards of knowledge, skills and understanding required for any given grade will be awarded that grade. Irrespective of how well or badly their peers have done. Grading standards are also constant from year to year. Performance which would have merited a C grade last year will yield the same grade this year.*[16]

Teachers know this to be Machiavellian bunkum.

With the demise of strict criterion-referencing it is now impossible to compare standards from one year to the next. It undermines quality control, invalidates league tables and disguises the year-on-year success of teachers.

Conclusion

> *I feel very strongly that this system, apparently designed to give students more choice and a broader field of knowledge, has done exactly the opposite.*[17]

Of course, exam boards will give strategies to sidestep difficulties and say that flexibility is still possible with astute juggling, but why should teachers spend valuable time trying to circumvent a bad syllabus? Where is the backbone of these guardians of standards that they cannot stand up to an ill-informed quango and insist on structures of educational worth. If they fear for their jobs now, where will they be if everyone opts for the International Baccalaureate?

In the light of my initial experience of the new specifications, I suggest that the QCA and exam boards contemplate the following:

- A separate course which allows for sustained study at greater depth for those planning, from the start, to continue to A2.
- A condensed course for those wishing only to pursue art for one year with built-in time to experiment and to develop, with some rigour, burgeoning strengths without the need to hit a wide variety of superficial targets. This would mean less product: dare I say it, a similar exam to the old Advanced Supplementary.
- The achievement of an A grade at A2 should not be dependent on an A grade at AS level, or an aggregate score.
- It should be possible to build upon AS work at A2, without the need for replication, to instill some semblance of professional working practice.
- Art should continue to be assessed holistically to allow students to explore their limitations, work to their strengths and push at boundaries without fear of prejudice.

Since governments of either persuasion have tended to adhere to Kenneth Clarke's dictum that 'education is too important to be left to educationalists', I suppose my plea to Blair, Adonis, Wicks *et al.* to heed Piaget will fall on deaf ears. Nevertheless, it is as true of lawmakers as it is of children that understanding involves the 'assimilation' of new information gained through experience; and 'accommodation' the altering of existing understandings to accept and act upon new information.

By prescribing more you will end up with less.

Carpe Diem.

Originally published in the *Journal of Art and Design Education* 21.1, 2002.

References

1. Taylor, R (2000), personal letter to John Steers.
2. Pasmore, V (1959), publication unknown.
3. Serota, N (2000), 'Who's Afraid of Modern Art?' Richard Dimbleby Lecture.
4. Barrett, M (1979), *Art Education: a strategy for course design*, London: Heinemann.
5. Steers, J response to subject specifications consultation.
6. North London Collegiate School student.
7. Graham and Tytler (1993), *A Lesson For Us All: The Making of the National Curriculum*, London: Routledge.
8. Smith, P JF Kennedy Roman Catholic School, Hemel Hempstead.
9. The Gulbenkian Foundation, (1982), *The Arts in Schools: Principles, Practice and Provision*.
10. NSEAD, (1991), Response to the interim report of the national curriculum art working group, *Journal of Art and Design Education*, vol. 10, no. 2, p. 199.
11. Eisner, E (1973), *'Do Behavioural Objectives and Accountability Have a Place in Art Education?'*, *Art Education*, 26 no. 5.
12. Brace, A (2001), *Another Level But Is It Worth It? Times Educational Supplement*, 18 May.
13. Barrett, M (1979), *ibid*.
14. Dorn, C (1999), *Mind in Art, Cognitive Foundations in Art Education*, Lawrence Erlbaum Associates Publishers, p. 235.
15. Graham, M from a letter to Agnes DeMille. www.neverisapromise.com/niap/fa/influences.html.
16. Wicks, M (1999), letter to *The Independent on Sunday*, 21/2/99.
17. Williams, R (2001), Woldgate School, Pocklington, Yorks, letter to *The Independent* 17/5/01.

Chapter 5: Striving for appropriate, reliable and manageable vocational assessment

Sylvia Willerton

The era of the General National Vocational Qualifications (GNVQs) draws to a close in 2006[1] with the last summer examination for Intermediate and Foundation levels. GCSE Applied (Double Award) has already replaced GNVQ Part 1; the first subject awards took place in June 2004. Advanced Vocational Certificate of Education (VCE), which superseded Advanced Level GNVQ in 2000, will be re-launched as a GCE Applied qualification with teaching programmes commencing in September 2005. The main drive for this ongoing development had been to achieve parity of esteem for vocational qualifications through the implementation of an appropriate assessment regime. To put these new qualifications into context, particularly in light of the Tomlinson recommendations for 14-19 Curriculum and Qualifications reform, it is useful to reflect on the original GNVQ model and the successive reviews and changes that have taken place over its lifespan.

On its introduction in 1992, GNVQ had seemed a radical concept in British education and assessment, which challenged traditional ideas and well-established assessment principles and practices. It highlighted the tensions and divisions that existed between education and training, academic and professional practice and formative and summative assessment. It also fuelled the debate about educational 'standards', the reliability and validity of assessment and parity between vocational and academic qualifications.[2] From a historical background of autonomous development of different vocational qualifications from an array of organizations, GNVQ, as Ecclestone argues

> *...emerged rapidly from the low status margins of vocational educational policy and a short-lived immunity from political interference, to become enmeshed in what might be described as an ideological and epistemological maelstrom around assessment.*[3]

Add to this turmoil, the conflicting agendas of key stakeholders and serious underfunding of implementation, it is not surprising that GNVQ development was thwarted by problems, often confused and constantly undermined. The original model had flaws, but many of the issues were exacerbated by increasing demands for external assessment by government and the opposing interests of the different organizations involved in policy.[4] GNVQs were introduced to raise the status of vocational education by replacing the confusing range of Post-16 qualifications with a coherent system that would provide a high-quality alternative to GCE A Levels and a viable route into higher education.[5] However, metamorphic changes to the model resulted in its identity, position and purpose being less clearly defined.

The intention to introduce the GNVQ was first announced in the Government White Paper 'Education and Training for the 21st Century' in May 1991. The structure was drafted in the summer of that year, and a consultation exercise involving 500 organizations was carried out by NCVQ. From the questionnaires returned the result was a convincing 93 per cent support for the introduction of GNVQs from schools, colleges, employers and awarding bodies. Ninety per cent felt that the emphasis should be on testing competence by continual assessment, as with NVQs, rather than testing knowledge with end-of-course examinations, the main characteristics of GCE A Levels. More than 60 per cent were opposed to centrally set tests. Of those who did favour them, the main reason was as a means of achieving parity with GCE A Levels. The feedback from the consultation helped to shape the initial specifications. GNVQs, as NVQs, consisted of a series of units; for example, Level 3 was composed of eight mandatory vocational units, four optional units and three Core Skill units. These were internally assessed and internally and externally verified. Units were individually accredited; therefore students who left courses before completing the full award still had recognition for the units they had completed.

Research carried out concurrently with the delivery and development of GNVQ Art and Design as it unfolded, with a range of centres from FE and the school sector across the three awarding bodies, suggested that GNVQ, as a learning approach, was effective; student motivation being a key feature.[6] The majority of the students interviewed preferred the new style and focus of delivery and appreciated their increased independence in decision-making. Aspects of the courses that had met with particular approval had been:

- the opportunity to work with a wide range of media, materials and processes;
- visits to craft workshops, design studios and galleries;
- work experiences in art, craft or design-based employment;
- increased time in the subject area.

A number of art and design teachers and lecturers had observed an increase in self-confidence, commitment and enthusiasm amongst their GNVQ students. Some had commented that their vocational students had compared well with GCE A Level students both in the quality of the practical work they produced and their attitude to work and progression. It had also been noticeable how well many students had functioned as part of a team. Although the general philosophy and vocational focus of GNVQ had appealed to both art and design students and teaching staff, concerns had been expressed about a number of obstacles that had interfered with the smooth running of their courses. For example,

- there was a deep-rooted perception that vocational qualifications were for less able students and did not have the status of academic qualifications. Even a cursory glance at the specifications would have dispelled such a notion.
- the end of unit mastery tests, which were only a small component of the overall qualification had taken on an inflated importance as their passing was a statutory requirement, yet their theoretical content bore only superficial relevance to the unit's requirements.
- the detailed recording of evidence for assessment had been excessive and time consuming. It had often been exacerbated by generic 'in-house' documentation systems imposed by some centres, which were incompatible with the type of work produced in art and design.

Initial problems relating to the complexity of the language used in the specifications and the imbalance between content requirements for different units had been partially addressed in the revisions of 1993 and later in 1995. The GNVQ levels were also renamed Foundation, Intermediate and Advanced, which appeared to distance them from NVQs, and the Core Skill units were renamed Key Skills. However, flaws in the assessment regime remained.

The grading criteria were generic, which led inevitably to different interpretations. Three grading themes, *Planning, Information Seeking and Handling* and *Evaluation*, referred to the completion of a process, but not specifically to the quality of the work produced. This caused a predicament for Art and Design assessors, which led to inconsistencies. To separate artificially the quality of the visual communication from the intentions would be anomalous, as they are interdependent. It is the quality and use of visual language that dictates whether creative ideas and intentions are in fact recognized and understood by others. The final grade would also be meaningless for progression, therefore, some centres interpreted quality as being implicit in the grading themes, while others did not.[7] This was addressed, to some extent, by the introduction of the fourth grading theme, '*Quality of Outcomes*' in 1994, but some inconsistency remained, often compounded by non-subject specific verifiers applying their own notion of 'weighting' to the evidence required for the themes, which skewed the vocational focus of the qualification. For example, non-subject specialist attached more importance to written communication skills as evidence of planning, as opposed to the intrinsic evidence of the planning process in the practical work because they did not possess, to use an Eisner term, the '*connoisseurship*'[8] to recognize it, or the continuous selection, modification and evaluation in the creative process, described by Schön as '*reflection-in-action*',[9] therefore more weight was placed on the candidate's performance in generic tasks rather than competence in the vocational area. At some centres the whole verification process had been carried out by non-subject specific internal *and* external verifiers.[10] At the other extreme, there was evidence of subject-specific verifiers ignoring evidence submitted for the key skill units. Alison Wolfe raised similar issues of inconsistency in relation to NVQs in 1995.[11] NCVQ were aware of different practices, but did not hold statutory powers to impose changes on the awarding bodies, but only to strongly recommend. In March 1994, Tim Boswell, Under-Secretary of State for Further and Higher Education, set out a six-point agenda for action. This included ensuring that external verifiers had '*...appropriate subject expertise*'[12] but this was not fully enforced until 2000. As GNVQs were introduced as general qualifications, but with *specific* vocational performance criteria, it would seem justifiable to have had specific grading criteria for the vocational subject area, identified under the generic grading theme titles, without compromising the model. It would also have removed a loophole that generic criteria somehow justified the use of non-subject specific verifiers. I raised this with NCVQ in 1993, but such a measure was considered incompatible, as it would move away from the principle of the generic model. However, in practice, course leaders, students, assessors and verifiers had to translate the generic terminology and apply it to a specific vocational context, which, led to inconsistency in interpretation. The introduction of a mandatory standardization process for assessment and grading would also have increased reliability and help to maintain parity and standards across the units, centres and over time.

The externally set end-of-unit mastery tests (short answer tests in 1992, which changed to multiple choice questions in 1993) had not been part of the original policy proposal. Gilbert Jessup, Director of GNVQ Research and Development at NCVQ argued, in 1991, that '*along with the new standards must go new forms of assessment very different from sitting examinations*', and that assessment should facilitate '*learning rather than acting as a deterrent or just an obstacle to be overcome*'. He reasoned:

> *...we must not persist in viewing assessment as we have, often quite rightly in the past, as an unwanted addition to the process of learning which distorts the aim of the curriculum. In the new model assessment is a natural and integral part of the learning process.*[13]

Ministerial pressure for external testing resulted in the swift formulation of test specifications in the summer of 1992.[14] The flaws in 'bolt-on' assessment became apparent to me and other NCVQ consultants as we attempted to identify the types of knowledge and understanding essential to the Elements, Performance Criteria and Range Statements in each of the units. For example, the evidence indicators in Element 1, Unit 4, *Evaluate influences on art and design* required

> *An exploration of current influences on art and design outcomes.*
> *A critical appraisal of own work analysing current influences on it.*[15]

This was essentially a subjective experience, dependent on the creative development of a student's own ideas. The current influences and the types of outcome would be as diverse as the number of GNVQ candidates.

The range requirements for this element were

> *Cultural influences; own culture, others' cultures, multi-cultures.*
> *Historical influences; industrial, economic, social, political, philosophical, psychological.*[16]

This gave endless scope for students to research *any* cultural or historical sources that were of interest to them and related to their own field of study and for course tutors to choose any art, craft or design movements or developments in which their own particular expertise lay. As a GNVQ was a specification of standards of achievement and *not* a syllabus, this method of external assessment was not only inappropriate for the qualification itself, but was ineffective in reflecting any depth of knowledge and understanding of art and design practice. To produce mastery test specifications to cover such a vast range of specialist knowledge would be excessive to say the least. To make the specifications so generic as to accommodate all possible avenues of study would inevitably be based on the lowest common denominators. This suggested that the motive for imposing the end of unit tests had more to do with the traditional notion, that written tests implied rigour and therefore accountable external assessment was *seen* to take place, than concern for the validity of the assessment itself. Broadfoot argues that the association of status with written examinations can be traced back to the qualifying examinations for professionals such as doctors, solicitors and accountants in the nineteenth century.

> *Since these examinations were associated with high status professions, the model of the written theoretical test they used became invested with a similar high status – a status it still retains.*[17]

However, a motive for the institution of those early professional examinations had been to ensure exclusivity, thus limiting access to the professions. In effect this had been a license to practice, in contrast to more recent vocational qualifications designed to promote more accessibility.

High-profile dissatisfaction with these tests resulted in development being concentrated on their reform, rather than the assessment regime as a whole. The subject advisory committee at NCVQ felt that this form of testing was inappropriate for Art & Design where the synthesis of knowledge, skill and understanding is best expressed by practice. The committee considered that nothing could be gained from attempting to rationalize the existing tests and that they should be abandoned. The representative from the DFE had insisted that although there had to be some form of external assessment to ensure consistency, the Department had not stipulated what particular form the assessment should take. As the timescale was too tight to develop an alternative for courses starting in September 1994, the tests that had proved to be the most problematical, those for Advanced units 3, 6, 7 and 8 and Intermediate unit 3, were suspended until a more appropriate method of assessment could be implemented.

As a member of the Subject Advisory Committee and a consultant at NCVQ, I was involved in exploring several alternative models for the testing of Advanced unit 7, *Working to set design briefs*. A developmental trial of three of the models took place in April and May 1995 with eighteen participating centres. Briefly they were:

- a case study approach; a 1½-hour short answer paper based on an illustrated case study
- a task-based examination; a 1-hour short answer paper, which followed a two-hour, non-assessed practical response to an externally set brief
- a practical task; a 4-hour practical examination in response to an externally set brief

Overall, the participating centres had been positive and optimistic, considering all three models to be an improvement on the multiple-choice tests. Some centres, however, had reservations about increased time and workload implications, particularly if similar models were to be used for other unit tests; a situation, which would be compounded by a build-up of possible retakes. Consultants had suggested that one test could easily incorporate the criteria for two or more units. Most students and staff who participated in the task-based model felt that the practical work should have been assessed in conjunction with the written responses. The case study approach was rejected by the awarding bodies on financial grounds and the practical task had been considered as a drain on centres' resources. An operational pilot of the task-based model, managed jointly by the three awarding bodies (BTEC, CGLI and RSA), was carried out between November 1995 and March 1996 involving 39 centres. Three different combinations of internal and external assessment were used, and, as in the previous trial, the practical work did not form part of the assessment.

The Dearing Report, reviewing the National Curriculum, recommended that a vocational pathway should be developed that would maintain a broad educational component at Key Stage 4, as part of a 14-19 continuum.[18] As a result, a Part 1 GNVQ was developed by SCAA and NCVQ and managed jointly by the three awarding bodies. The Art and Design specification was introduced at the second phase in 1996. As in the full award, there was a requirement to pass the unit mastery tests. In addition, extension unit tests assisted in the determination of the grades. At Intermediate level all three extension tests were a combination of short-answer and practical responses. At Foundation level the extension tests for Unit A, *Exploring 2D techniques*, and Unit B, *Exploring 3D techniques*, were fixed response papers, while Unit C, *Investigating working in art, craft and design*, was a short-answer paper.[19] Foundation candidates were often those with weaker written communication skills, yet the test specifications gave no opportunity to include practical responses. As a quality assurance measure, centres were also required to include an externally set controlled assignment in the first year of the GNVQ programme. This added up to an excessive amount of external testing.

As the new model GNVQ specifications scheduled for September 2000 would also replace the Part 1 qualification, an interim assessment model was introduced specifically for the 1999 cohort. The Interim Model had one differentiated test, covering Pass, Merit and Distinction for each of the vocational units, which replaced the mastery and extension tests. The set assignment was also discontinued. Candidates had to achieve at least a pass in all three tests to gain the qualification. The Art and Design tests, for both Foundation and Intermediate levels, were a combination of short answers and practical responses to pre-seen briefs and images. Initially there had been some concern expressed by centres and Part 1 examiners that yet another change before September 2000 would cause unnecessary disruption. However, this concern had been outweighed by the overall reduction in external assessment.

NCVQ commissioned an independent review of GNVQ assessment and grading, particularly in relation to the revisions introduced in September 1995. The review, chaired by John Capey, was carried out over a five-month period in the same year. The report supported the distinctive characteristics, philosophy and structure of the qualification, for example, the promotion of an active learning process centred on the portfolio of evidence. However, a number of concerns were identified relating to the manageability of the assessment demands; the delivery and assessment of key skills; grading procedures and the purpose and quality of the external tests.[20] As a result of the recommendations, a pilot of selected units was undertaken for two terms during the 1996/97 academic year, from September to March, in three vocational areas: Art and Design, Business and Health and Social Care. Although the subject content remained the same, a simplified unit structure was used, together with revised grading criteria (using just two grading themes, *Learning Skills* and *Quality of Outcome*, both of equal weighting), along with a different style of external tests and set assignments. The development of the latter drew on the experiences of the Part 1 pilot. It also incorporated ideas that had emerged from the 1995 trial, for example, the Advanced test covered the criteria of two units. Therefore, the significant change was that of purpose, which was to assess the *application* of vocational skills, knowledge and understanding rather than confirmation of a broad knowledge and understanding of the unit range in the existing tests.

The model was superseded in September 1997 by the 'New Model' pilot. The new model GNVQ was designed to encompass the recommendations of the Dearing review of qualifications for 16- to 19-year-olds published in March 1996. The significant difference between the two reviews had been that, whilst Capey had focused on reducing the assessment burden, Dearing had proposed an increase in external assessment to secure rigour.[21] The assessment regime used in the Art and Design pilot drew on features of the GNVQ Assessment Review pilot and the Part 1 assessment models. There was a considerable shift in the balance of assessment demand as a result of a disproportionate emphasis on the assessment of the key skill units. For example, Application of number had a multiple-choice test, a set assignment *and* portfolio assessment, which gave it an inflated importance over the vocational units. Concerns had been raised by pilot centres that the time spent on preparing for, and taking the vocational and key skill tests along with assignments, had dramatically reduced the time available for producing portfolio evidence – the crux of the qualification. This ultimately impinged on the style of course delivery and opportunities for independent learning. It is worth reiterating, a point raised in the Cockroft Report, 1982, that '*No-one has ever grown taller as a result of being measured*'.[22] In August 1998, Wolfe made a case for decoupling key skills from GNVQ.

> *What this ill-conceived pilot makes clear is the muddled nature of the whole key skill idea. If it is about applying existing skills, then the assessment regime is a nonsense. If it is about raising young people's level of written English, Mathematics, or software use, then we need a proper debate on what this age-group should be learning, ...the short term solution is clear enough: namely to uncouple key skills from the GNVQ, and allow the latter to develop as a coherent qualification.*[23]

QCA had been aware of the potential repercussions, Geoff Lucas, the Head of Corporate Policy, replied,

> *The Qualification and Curriculum Authority is looking carefully at the arguments for and against retaining key skills as a mandatory part of GNVQ, drawing on the findings of the pilot...the result of the pilot will strongly influence our final recommendations on how to make the new key skill qualification both manageable and rigorous.*[24]

Development of the subject criteria for GCE A and AS Level specifications in 1998 moved closer to the GNVQ domain. It seems ironic, that the excessive amount of external assessment introduced in the New Model pilot, might have become one of the main distinguishing features. In March 1999, towards the end of the second year of the pilot, the Government announced new reforms to Post-16 qualifications to be launched in 2000. As a result, the proposed changes to GNVQ assessment were put on hold.

When the revised specifications were introduced in 2000, along with the new GCE AS and A2 qualifications, the Advanced level GNVQ became Advanced VCE and any remaining association with NVQs disappeared. Although GNVQ Intermediate and Foundation levels had been scheduled to end, there had been many requests for their retention because, as the equivalent of four GCSEs, they provided valuable one-year Post-16 vocational courses for students staying on in full-time education who did not wish to enrol in A Level courses. DfES decided that they would be retained until suitable alternatives are available. The main changes to the assessment and grading process in VCE, which also applies to Intermediate and Foundation levels, include:

- The key skill units have been de-coupled from the qualification. Opportunities to complete the key skill units remain but they cease to be a mandatory requirement.
- The documentation of evidence for assessment, an intrinsic feature of GNVQ has been substantially simplified.
- The assessment requirements have been reduced. Each unit is now assessed by only one method, for example, candidates are not required to produce portfolio evidence for the externally tested units 4, 5 and 7.
- The multiple-choice tests have finally been replaced by external assessment that combines practical and written responses to a set brief.
- A five-scale grading system, A–E, has been adopted. This aligns VCE more closely with GCE grading. GNVQ Intermediate and Foundation retained the grading scale of Pass, Merit and Distinction.
- The generic grading themes have been replaced by grading criteria related to each individual unit.
- A mandatory requirement to use subject-specific moderators; an inconsistency in practice that had taken eight years to address.[25]

Although some assessment issues have been addressed and some parity of esteem with GCE may have been achieved, it has come at a price; the vocational content of VCE has diminished from that of Advanced GNVQ whilst changes in assessment have led to a more academic approach to delivery, leaving less flexibility for linking courses with work experience in art, craft and design-based employment. This had been an effective way of covering the GNVQ specifications, particularly Advanced Unit 5, *Business and Professional Practice*.[26] Similar issues applying to VCE qualifications in general have been identified by OFSTED.[27] It has become crucial for centres to maintain a strong vocational focus when planning their programmes and developing briefs, to distinguish VCE from GCE.

When GCSE Applied (Double Award) was introduced in September 2002 it replaced the three-unit GNVQ Part 1 specification, the equivalent to two GCSEs. It has similar features to VCE and assessment is more in line with the GCSE model. In contrast to GNVQ assessment, where candidates had to meet all the criteria for a Pass grade before moving to the Merit criteria, candidates can now achieve an uneven profile across the assessment marking criteria, so strengths can balance weaknesses. The combination of practical and written externally set and marked tests for each of the three Part 1 units have been replaced with an externally set assignment for Unit 3 '*Working to project briefs*'. Unit 1 '*2D and 3D visual language*' and Unit 2 '*Materials, techniques and technology*' are internally assessed portfolio units.[28] All three are externally moderated. So far there has been a positive response, with uptake from centres with experience of vocational qualifications and also those more familiar with GCSE. However, interviews with art and design teachers, in early 2004, delivering Applied courses and those planning future courses have highlighted some inconsistencies. In many centres it is being offered in the main option pattern and appropriate time is being given for a Double Award, while in others, timetable managers are treating it as a qualification for the less able and it is not being offered to higher ability groups. Some teachers felt that they were being given insufficient time to deliver a Double Award, which puts undue pressure on them and disadvantages their students. Similar inconsistencies in provision and access were prevalent in GNVQ, which suggests that qualifications may change, but general attitudes to parity of esteem between vocational and academic qualifications have not.

The final stage of metamorphosis takes place in September 2005 when VCE will emerge as an Applied GCE. It will have a single and Double Award with AS–A2 progression. Unlike GNVQ and VCE, where the mandatory units are common across awarding bodies, the new unit specifications have been devised by each awarding body and submitted to QCA for accreditation. In general the Art and Design content of VCE has been retained and has been separated to allow a general approach at AS level, and more specific vocational pathways at A2 level. External assessment will take the form of set assignments, internally assessed and externally moderated, as Applied GCSE and the GCE models. There will be no pre-determined grades for the portfolio units, which is current practice. If, and by how much, this new specification will be affected by Mike Tomlinson's recommendation to de-couple GCE AS and A2 to create two free-standing qualifications, remains to be seen.

Revisions, reforms and the debate will certainly continue. In 2001 the Government first proposed the introduction of a coherent 14-19 phase of education,[29], which will inevitably lead to the further development and expansion of vocational education. Attention was again drawn to the sharp distinction between academic and vocational learning opportunities in the English system in the DfES policy document '14–19, Opportunity and Excellence', 2003. It adds that a much stronger vocational offer is required, '*ensuring assessment within programmes is fit for purpose*' and cites concerns, raised during consultation in 2002, that changes to the assessment of vocational qualifications in recent years has '*constrained the learning styles to which many young people responded positively. This in turn reduced the impact of their programmes, and made them less accessible.*'[30] Tomlinson has taken this on board. The report on the '14–19 Curriculum and Qualifications Reform', October 2004, recommends a new framework of diplomas at Entry, Foundation, Intermediate and Advanced levels, with grading at Pass, Merit and Distinction (titles familiar with those involved in vocational education), which will encompass academic and vocational qualifications. The aims, again, are to raise the quality and status of vocational education and provide the same opportunities for progression as for those in academic studies. '*This does not mean trying to fit vocational programmes into an academic mould, but recognising what is distinctive and valuable about vocational learning and ensuring that it is respected and valued in its own right.*'[31]

Much will now depend on the Government's response to the final report expected in early 2005[32] and whether it can accept that different forms of assessment can be appropriate, reliable and manageable. Partial, or piecemeal, implementation of recommended reforms can skew the overall objectives, as happened with GNVQ. However, any major changes to assessment taken forward ought to be thoroughly trialled and tested before implementation, which has not always happened in the past.

References

1. *Time extended for retakes.*
2. Willerton, S (2001), *GNVQ Art and Design: The Development, Distortion and Subsequent Dismantling of its More Radical Features*, Ph.D. Thesis, University of Sussex.
3. Eccleston, K (1999), *Bewitched, Bothered and Bewildered*, paper presented to The British Educational Research Association Conference, University of Sussex.
4. *Ibid.*

5. Shepard, G (July 1992), *NCVQ News Release.*
6. Willerton, S *op. cit.* (2001).
7. *Ibid.*
8. Eisner, E (1979), *The Educational Imagination*, New York, Macmillan Publishing Co., Inc.
9. Schön, P A (1983), *The Reflective Practitioner, How Professionals Think in Action*, New York, Basic Books.
10. Willerton, S *op. cit.* (2001).
11. Wolf, A (1995), *Competence Based Assessment*, Buckingham, Open University Press.
12. Boswell, T (1994), *Letter to NCVQ.*
13. Jessup, G (1991), *Outcomes, NVQs and the Emerging Model of Education and Training*, London, Falmer Press.
14. Unpublished NCVQ *Guidance notes for consultants, (1992).*
15. GNVQ Art and Design, (1992), Level 3 Specifications.
16. *Ibid.*
17. Broadfoot, P (1979), *Assessment, School and Society*, London, Methuen & Co. Ltd.
18. Dearing, R (1993), *The National Curriculum and its Assessment*, London, SCAA.
19. GNVQ Art & Design, (1996), Part 1 Specifications.
20. Capey, J (1995), *GNVQ Assessment Review*, London, NCVQ.
21. Dearing, R (1996), *Review of Qualifications for 16–19 Year Olds*, London, SCAA.
22. The Cockroft Report, (1982), London, DES.
23. Wolf, A (1998), *Rotten Core could Kill*, TES, 14/08/98.
24. Lucas, G (1998), *Still Studying the Key Skills Question*, TES, 28/09/98.
25. VCE, Art and Design Specifications, 2000.
26. Willerton, S & Willerton, B S (1997), *Advanced GNVQ, Business and Professional Practice*, Basingstoke, Macmillan Press Ltd.
27. Her Majesty's Chief Inspector of Schools, March 2004, *Vocational A Levels: The First Two Years*, London, OFSTED.
28. GCSE Applied Art and Design (Double Award) Specifications, 2002.
29. Government Green Paper, (2001), *Schools Building on Success.*
30. Government Policy Document, (2003), *14–19 Opportunity and Excellence.*
31. Final Report of the Working Group, (October 2004), *14–19 Curriculum and Qualifications Reform*, DfES Publications.
32. This chapter was written in October 2004.

Chapter 6: Portfolio development in a secondary teaching credential art program

Mika Cho

For many years, portfolios have been used by artists to represent their works, to demonstrate artistic expression and competence, and to help them secure additional support for their work. The use of portfolios is not a particularly new or innovative assessment process in art. However, in fields such as teacher education, the use of portfolios with pre-service teachers is a fairly recent alternative assessment system.[1] A subject-specific portfolio is able to illustrate a student's goal setting, growth, achievement, and reflection.[2] Some researchers argue that teacher education has the responsibility of preparing pre-service teachers to use alternative assessment practices[3] rather than relying on standardized tests. Criticism of the traditional approaches to the assessment of pre-service teachers has led educators to portfolios as a form of authentic assessment.[4]

This article describes portfolio development by pre-service art teachers in a secondary teaching program at California State University, Los Angeles, United States of America. The article also addresses the questions of what a portfolio in art education is, what its goals are, how one creates a portfolio, how one assesses portfolios once they are developed, what the issues and challenges surrounding the use of portfolios as assessment tools are, and, finally, some likely future developments of portfolio assessment in teacher education.

What is a portfolio in art education?

The portfolio has been integrated as a capstone experience in the secondary teacher education program in art at California State University, Los Angeles since 1995. All single subject teaching credential students must take this course in the art education program. The development of a portfolio in art education is central to this course. Students gather and organize materials and document active learning in the teaching credential program to show knowledge of subject matter as well how to enhance student learning. The portfolio provides (i) for the faculty an authentic assessment tool, (ii) a self-assessment tool for pre-service teachers with a reflective picture of their work, and (iii) advantage beyond a simple resumé in the job application process.

The typical portfolio consists of a curriculum vitae, an autobiography including a statement of one's educational philosophy, national and state standard based art curriculum developed in the teaching methods course, art classroom observations written by the students, interviews with in-service art teachers in secondary education, articulated coursework and relevant extra curricula activities, a review of literature for relevant theories and practices in art teaching and learning, a description of directed student teaching preparation and practice, case studies, presentations, a list of professional organizations in which the student is a member, slides and photos of creative work or projects, academic transcripts, and, finally, letters of recommendation and recognition. Clearly, such a portfolio provides a much more comprehensive picture of a pre-service teacher than a simple resumé and a transcript of coursework.

Goals and objectives of portfolios in art education

The first question one should ask about the use of portfolios in art education is: "Why?" A portfolio can reflect knowledge, skills and beliefs about teaching art. It displays one's learning experiences as they are collected, organized and refined to provide a critical framework and rich portrayal of one's best work. In addition, the portfolio becomes a reflective tool. Taking courses, learning theories and practice in teaching are not enough without reflection. The portfolio forces the pre-service teacher to reflect on the profession of teaching and to answer the philosophical question of "why", and can represent an answer to this question. Too often, pre-service teachers go through the motions of learning about teaching without becoming committed to the profession, without seeing themselves as professionals. As a result, they do not fully understand what goes on in the art classrooms. Perhaps this is why beginning teachers in urban areas have a high attrition rate.

Without meaningful assessment, the process of teacher education is often mechanistic, unreflective and unrelated to the realities of teaching. The portfolio, however, makes a vital connection between the pre-service teacher and the urban classroom realities. For example, one of the assignments in developing a portfolio requires pre-service teachers to observe and interview practicing teachers. They must then reflect and analyze the experience and discuss their observations with peers to broaden their understanding of the actual classrooms. Developing an effective portfolio in art education benefits pre-service teachers and the faculty by identifying competency and knowledge of subject matter and teaching. One of the purposes of a portfolio in art education is to document pre-service teachers' growth and enable them to see themselves as successful and competent learners. A portfolio is much more than a collection or checklist of assignments or materials stuffed into a Manila folder or pasted into a scrapbook. Each piece of evidence in a portfolio must be collected or created and organized in a compelling manner to demonstrate proficiency in a skill or progress toward a goal. The portfolio provides reviewers with a comprehensive picture of pre-service teachers' work. It is also a self-assessment tool. It can be used during one's pre-service teacher education program to provide formative assessment and, at the conclusion of one's teacher education process, to demonstrate proficiency.

Creating the ideal portfolio in art education

There is no such thing as the 'perfect portfolio', but there are some guidelines for the quality and usefulness of a portfolio. One must develop a *cohesive format* for the portfolio's contents, in order to demonstrate the following competency areas. First and foremost is teaching and learning potential, then instructional methodology, subject matter knowledge, beliefs about and philosophy of teaching art, creative ability, knowledge of diverse cultures, and potential for social interaction within a variety of schools and community settings with diverse populations of students.

Also, a portfolio should be viewed as a 'work in progress', something that one continuously builds upon. Barton and Collins[5] state that

> *The ongoing nature of the portfolio development process gives both students and faculty an opportunity to reflect on student growth and change throughout the course of a program – an opportunity that does not exist with a one time, exit-oriented exam.*

Assessing portfolios

The question the reviewer faces is how to assess several portfolios at hand. One hopes to transcend pure subjective judgement and move toward the high ground of objectivity. In reviewing the work of Erwin,[6] Pedras[7] highlights the following distinction:

> *Addressing this issue, Erwin compares two techniques, the 'selected-response' and 'constructed-response' assessment techniques, distinguishing them by calling the former a recognition format and the latter a production format. He also quotes several authors as saying that the multiple choice, true-false, and matching questions that make up selected-response techniques are viable measures of how much learning has taken. To demonstrate the constructed response technique, an example is given in which a dance major would be expected to perform before an audience as part of the assessment process. While the selected-response technique is suitable to measure some things, it falls short when it is used to assess learning in areas such as painting or sculpture. It's all very well to assess a sculptor's knowledge of metal-casting or rock types, or a painter's ability to mix colors, but the accomplishment of both of these people is measured by the quality of the creation that is a result of adding creative ability to technological expertise. The quality of a sculpture can't be measured by a true-false test. In fact the ability to produce something can only be predicted with the standard selected-response techniques; it can't be measured in this way and that is why the portfolio (the quintessential constructed response) is used in assessment of performance.*

Clearly, there is a parallel with teaching excellence in the above. Knowing learning theories and sound pedagogical approaches does not insure that an individual will be a great or even good teacher. In addition to 'knowing', sound teaching requires action and successful interaction with students.

Pedras is helpful, but his distinction does not go far enough in capturing the assessment of a complex portfolio. Portfolios must demonstrate both learning and the potential to perform in a classroom *over an extended period of time*. It is perhaps useful to look at the intended purpose of the portfolio in light of its function during and after a student's preparatory education.

Portfolios as process (formative) tools

For a portfolio to improve the student's educational experience, it should include the following elements: progress of the development of values and beliefs related to teaching and learning; knowledge and skills connected with one's teaching philosophy; developed and refined observation skills; applications of acquired knowledge to teaching and learning; problem-solving, decision-making and leadership skills; and proficiency in authentic assessment techniques.

Portfolios as product (summative) tools

When the purpose of the portfolio is to document the culmination of students' educational preparation, the following criteria should be considered: a refined presentation of achievement that is more than transcripts or test scores; a chronicle of professional and personal growth across stages of learning and teaching; personal standards of excellence established during pre-service teaching; a demonstration of professional skills for teaching in the future; and evidence of the student's potential to be an effective art teacher in a classroom.

The assessment for the portfolio pilot project at California State University, Los Angeles had two components. The first was the evaluation of the approach used in the course (developing and using portfolios). The second component was the development and use of a set of rubrics for scoring and rating the different parts of a portfolio. The evaluation of the approach in developing and using portfolios focused on students' reactions to portfolios as a learning tool as compared to more traditional forms of assessment (such as exams and reports). Some evaluation questions also explored the reasons for their preferences. The second assessment component consisted of developing and using rubrics to capture students' progress in their learning. Separate rubrics were developed for each of the major parts of a portfolio.

In the pilot project, the strategy used for assessing portfolio quality was firstly that the portfolio contents and rubrics were agreed upon by the faculty and pre-service teachers before the work began. Secondly, each assignment in the course was coordinated to eventually become a component of a portfolio, with continuous feedback on its development. Thirdly, a set of criteria was used to review every portfolio. Once the portfolios were completed, they were graded on organization, aesthetics, creativity, a demonstrated knowledge of the teaching profession, content mastery, classroom organization and management and overall cohesiveness. The ultimate goal of the portfolio in this course was developmental – it helped pre-service teachers become more focused on their future profession and developed their capacity for self-assessment and reflection. Consequently, the project dealt with both the process (formative) and the product (summative).

Lessons learned

The pilot study revealed several lessons which can benefit others interested in using portfolio. First, it revealed the need to re-examine the art education teaching credential program. Clearly, the portfolios drew upon students' work throughout their teaching credential program, including the work in prior courses. In short, what was measured was more than what was achieved in the one course. While this may not necessarily be bad, it did complicate grading for the course.

Secondly, portfolios reassured students about their teaching careers, and its preparation. Without portfolios and the reflection it provided, students may not have felt as confident about entering the teaching profession. Before this pilot, there was no 'culminating' course to help them put all of their work and preparation together, but only a series of separately graded courses. This was a major benefit for the students.

Thirdly, several issues and challenges emerged related to the assessment of portfolios once they were completed. These are discussed in the next section.

Challenges to portfolio assessment

There still remain a number of unanswered questions and challenges to using portfolios for assessment. There is an assumption that portfolio assessment will provide a 'better' indication of overall teaching potential. This issue remains arguable amongst educators. While portfolios *can* provide a richer picture of subject matter knowledge, instructional methodology, internship experiences and the ability to organize and present lessons, it is not clear they always do. When applied to teaching performance, portfolio assessment may not be as useful as it is when applied to artistic ability. This is because *successful teaching and learning* goes beyond the performance of one individual; it involves the effective interaction between a teacher and a group of students over time. In fact, this group of students may come from diverse cultures and have different learning styles. Adding to the complexity, typically (in Los Angeles) the composition of the group of students changes year to year. In summary, the complexity of measuring the effectiveness of an individual's interactions with a large group is great.

Much of the literature on portfolios explores the potential of this assessment tool and focuses on contents and goals of portfolios. Research remains scarce on portfolio validity and reliability. In other words, few researchers have taken the time and made effort to demonstrate that portfolios for teachers are superior assessment tools. Do we know, for example, whether or not the objective ratings by faculty observers of student performance are effective? Can students ever be objective about their own work? Since students have control over the contents of a portfolio, there is nothing to stop them from selecting only the most favorable evidence for inclusion, while omitting the negative performance evidence.

Another question concerns inter-reviewer reliability of different portfolio reviewers. Since the assessment of portfolios involves the holistic impressions of the different reviewers, their conclusions about what constitutes a good and a bad teaching portfolio may not agree. Some effort must be made to ensure reviewers share the same criteria for judging portfolios. Criteria for judging portfolios need to be developed completely outside of and independent of portfolios themselves. Furthermore, such criteria need to be agreed upon beforehand by all of the potential reviewers or users of this assessment tool. As an example of this subjectivism, Adams[8] states that

> *some teacher educators might opt to grade portfolios on some basis (e.g., quality of products, quantity of products, etc.) while others might opt to use the assessment information collected to complement some other form of graded assessment. The choice to grade or not to grade and the scale for grading rests completely on the purpose for which portfolios are used.*

Elbow[9] discusses the reliability and validity of portfolio scoring. He argues that portfolios are an extremely valid form of assessment because they accurately measure the complex variables that contribute to students' real abilities, but this same complexity makes it difficult to reach reliable agreement among graders. Given the choice of achieving accuracy or maintaining clear standards across assessments, Elbow feels it makes more sense to focus on validity and allow reliability to suffer. Of course this argument flies in the face of sound psychometric reasoning since it stands to reason that any unreliable measurement instrument cannot deliver valid measures! Furthermore, Elbow misses the point about students selecting only their 'best' work for inclusion in the portfolio. Imagine how invalid a traditional test would be if students got to choose (and be graded on) only items they felt they could best answer and ignore all of the rest.

Another criticism of portfolio assessment is that there are certain organizational skills and presentation skills that come into play in putting a portfolio together. Students who are highly skilled in such areas may not necessarily be the best teachers, but know how to put together impressive portfolios. This again raises the question of validity.

Also, a student may be able to prepare and teach a brilliant lesson but may not be able to sustain such quality day in and day out. Teaching well is not a one-shot effort but rather a sustained effort over a long period of time. Since there may never be an adequate substitute for placing pre-service teachers in teaching positions for a probationary period and seeing how well they fare, portfolios should be used in addition to practice teaching.

Another issue is the cost benefit: Is the amount of time it takes to develop and prepare a comprehensive portfolio justified? Might there be another quicker method of demonstrating proficiency than the portfolio and how important is the time factor? Much work remains to be done before these issues are resolved and the use of portfolios for summative assessment is proven.

Conclusions and the future of portfolios

Portfolios represent a richer assessment format than traditional testing, grades or comprehensive exams. With increased use and familiarity of a portfolio as an assessment tool, the current challenges and obstacles to questions about their reliability and validity will eventually be answered. Once such questions have been answered, it is quite possible that portfolios will supplant the traditional curriculum vitae and coursework transcripts as selection criteria for teaching positions. On the other hand, many educators tend to be conservative, and while they readily flirt with notions like authentic assessment and portfolios, whether or not they ultimately incorporate them in the profession must await the test of time.

Finally, portfolios can provide an important reflection tool for students to think holistically about and to organize the work they have accomplished in a teaching credential program comprised of many separately graded courses. The potential for building future teachers' confidence about their preparation for their chosen careers may well be one of the most important reasons for using portfolios.

Originally published in the *Journal of Art and Design Education* 18. 2, 1999.

Notes and references

1. Centra, J A (1994), The use of the teaching portfolio and student evaluations for summative evaluation, *Journal of Higher Education*, 65(5), 555–570.
2. Adamchik, C F Jr (1995), Idea bank, *Science Teacher*, 62(7), p.58.
3. Stahle, D L & Mitchell, J P (1993), Portfolio assessment in college methods courses: Practicing what we preach, *Journal of Reading,* 36(7), pp.538–542.
4. Centra, *op. cit.*, Fontana, J (1995), Portfolio assessment: Its beginning in Vermont and Kentucky, *NASSP Bulletin*, 79(573), pp.25–30; Shannon, D M (1994), An Evaluation Approach for the Development of Pre-service Teachers, ED378183, p.20.
5. Barton, J & Collins, A (1993), Portfolio in teacher education, *Journal of Teacher Education*, 44(3), p.201.

6. Erwin, T D (1991), *Assessing student learning and development*, San Francisco: Jossey-Bass.
7. Pedras, M J (1994), Portfolio development and assessment in a teacher preparation program, ED382571, paper presented at the International Conference on Assessing Quality in Higher Education, 14, p.3.
8. Adams, T L (1995), A paradigm for portfolio assessment in teacher education, *Education*, 115(4), p.570.
9. Elbow, P (1991), Foreword in Belanoff, P & Dickson, M (eds.), *Portfolio: Process and Product*, Portsmouth, N.H.: Boynton/Cook.

Chapter 7: (In defence of) whippet-fancying and other vices: Re-evaluating assessment in art and design

Richard Hickman

Introduction

Whippets are traditionally the favoured racing dog – being a kind of elfin greyhound – amongst working-class males from the north of England. Judging whippets' ability to perform in a race is often based on a kind of connoisseurship, an almost magical facility to determine ability by judging apparently insignificant and barely discernable features, such as muscle tone or a determined gaze. I refer to this as a 'vice' not because of overtones of unnatural fondness for animals, but because of the pervasive requirement in education for clearly discernable and, therefore, measurable, qualities in things in order for them to have any currency. I first encountered the term in conversation with the late Professor Brian Allison, who used it disparagingly to refer to the use of connoisseurship in classroom research and also to the prevalence of the 'gut reaction' approach in the assessment of art and design.

The connoisseur – the expert – is someone who has studied something, perhaps informally, and has become intimately acquainted with all of its characteristics. The paradigm example is that of the art historian. It is ironic then that the expertise, and therefore professionalism, of art *educators* is challenged by taking away this facility and replacing it with externally set and formalized modes of assessment. There is a notion that everything that exists, exists in some quantity and can therefore be measured. This might well be true, but why would one wish to? Elliot Eisner's epigram before his discussion on the educational uses of assessment and evaluation in the arts is apposite here: 'Not everything that matters can be measured, and not everything that is measured matters'[1].

In researching for this chapter, I came across some old lecture notes, where I had written:

> *...assessment is not a bolt-on activity or something to be done at the end of an activity, but is integral to teaching and learning. Therefore it must be planned for and structured to ensure it maximises students' attainment and achievement.*

Although to many, the above might seem innocuous enough, I feel slightly embarrassed to have promulgated assessment in this way. The very phrasing 'it must be planned for and structured' makes me cringe slightly in the knowledge that art and design activities are often, by their very nature, unplanned and learning can emerge which was unintended and intended learning can often be fairly superficial. The idea of 'maximizing' students' attainment makes them seem more like factory farmed beasts rather than thinking, creative individuals. Further reading of my old notes revealed the following:

Before assessing students' work it is important to clarify ***why*** *the work is being assessed and also* ***what*** *is being assessed – Is it attitude? Creativity? Aesthetic sensitivity? Technical skill? Neatness? Originality? Or something else altogether?*

I have fewer problems with this. In various classrooms and at examination meetings, I have often heard teachers confess to using assessment as a means of control; others, sadly, do indeed value neatness over all else. Some see 'originality' as the most important aspect of artistic endeavour, regardless of that most elusive of concepts, quality. Each of these aspects needs to be dealt with in its own way; it is not desirable, for example, to assess technical skill in the same way as aesthetic sensitivity. I will argue that some aspects of learning in art and design should not be assessed at all, but that those aspects should be 'upgraded' while the role of assessment be 'demoted'. Firstly, a few words on different approaches to assessment, so as to put the arguments into context.

Approaches to assessment

Assessment can be thought of as an 'umbrella' concept, covering evaluation, testing, measuring, grading, examination and the general appraisal of achievement. Evaluation refers to judging the value of something and usually deals with qualitative aspects of performance; it tends to refer to the appraisal of curricular content. Testing refers to a process for obtaining data, while measuring deals with quantification, and grading is usually concerned with assigning a symbol which stands for a judgement of quality. Examination refers to a formal process whereby a student's achievement over a specified period of time in a particular place is measured against stated criteria. Achievement refers to the overall accomplishments of a student (including personal factors). All of these terms in the context of general education can be seen as discrete subdivisions of assessment.

The status of art and design in education relies to some extent upon its accountability. Assessing students' achievement in art and design within the context of an internationally recognized examination gives the subject credibility in the eyes of those who would otherwise see it as a fringe activity. Summative assessment occurs at the end of a project or course of study and therefore focuses on finished outcomes or more holistically on a body of work; it can be a culmination of evaluations made over a period of time. The principal means of summative assessment in England at the end of compulsory schooling is through the General Certificate of Secondary Education (GCSE) examination. The GCSE examination in art & design, in all of its various manifestations, has many positive qualities. It has been claimed to assess the following:

- intuitive and imaginative abilities;
- critical and analytical faculties;
- the ability to identify and solve problems in visual and tactile form;
- the ability to research, select, make and evaluate in a continuum;
- the ability to organize and relate abstract notions to practical outcomes;
- students' awareness and appreciation of relationships between art and design and the individual within the historical, social and environmental context;
- students' acquisition of a relevant subject specific working vocabulary;
- individuals' subject-specific special aptitudes and interests;
- students' understanding of economic considerations in the inventive use of materials and techniques.

Additionally, the examination is designed to foster and encourage confidence, enthusiasm and a sense of achievement. These are all very worthy, but whether the examination actually does assess or even facilitate these things is another matter. A fundamental principle that the GCSE examination was designed to assess is what school students know, understand and can do – in other words, it assesses what students are capable of, not what they are incapable of. In this respect, it is, I would suggest, a worthwhile procedure.

Formative assessment is usually continuous throughout the process of a particular learning activity. It has been recognized by most art and design educators that formative assessment is particularly constructive. It is concerned with providing ongoing feedback during the process of making rather than assessing and grading an isolated finished product. Formative assessment at its best is assessment *for* learning as well as *of* learning and plays an integral part in the development of projects; it encourages and guides the students' work forward. It is axiomatic that if students do not receive regular positive feedback on their work they can quickly lose motivation and become unsure of their own assessment of success or failure. It is therefore important to find approaches which build formative assessment consciously into practice so that its full potential can be explored, thus enhancing art and design teaching and students' learning.

Developmental (sometimes known as 'ipsative') assessment gauges the development of an individual from one moment in time to another (usually the present). It is concerned with the evaluation of personal achievement rather than an individual's relationship to national or local norms. Additionally students' self-assessment provides teachers with insights into students' understanding of their own progress. This can be used for diagnostic assessment. In short, developmental assessment reinforces positive qualities, comparing a students' present performance with past performances. It is concerned with individuals' growth and development; because developmental or ipsative assessment is intrinsically learner-centred, it is made by negotiation between teacher and taught and often takes the form of student self-assessment. This provides an opportunity for students to appraise themselves in a non-competitive climate.

Diagnostic assessment approaches students' work and behaviour as evidence for the analysis of their ability in a given field (it is often used to discover learning needs). It can be used constructively as a vehicle for discussion between teacher and student, where both parties consider progress, perhaps defining targets for future development. It can be a powerful motivating factor for students. Negotiated assessment in the form of constructive criticism promotes learning and a degree of student ownership in the assessment process.

Issues arising...

Not too long ago, there was a debate within art(s) education in Britain about whether assessment was a necessary evil, a generally good thing or something which will tear the soul out of art. The very title of Malcolm Ross's edited book *Assessment in Arts Education – A Necessary Discipline or a Loss of Happiness?* sums up the polarized views of the 1980s.[2] The 'loss of happiness' to which Ross refers is a reference to Charles Darwin's autobiography, where Darwin laments his lack of 'higher aesthetic faculties', blaming a lifetime of analysis and measurement for the consequent 'loss of happiness'[3]. Ross fulminated against the increasing incidence of measurement in education as away of legitimizing arts activities, as if an activity was not worthy if it could not be measured. The view that the legitimacy given by formal examinations to art and design is spurious, adversely affecting the inherent character of the subject, remains worthy of attention and is discussed further below.

The Education Reform Act of 1988 and the introduction of the national curriculum in England and Wales appeared to render such debate superfluous – it became a legal obligation for teachers to assess, record and report on their students' performance at regular intervals. Since 1997, in England and Wales, there has been a statutory requirement for teachers to assess non-core [e.g. art and design] subjects. Teachers are required to summarize their assessment for each student in year 9 (who is reaching the end of what has become known in England and Wales as Key Stage 3) in terms of a judgement of their attainment in relation to the end of key stage description for the attainment target.[4] In art and design, teachers are expected to make a judgement about the extent to which students have met the end of key stage descriptions and report their findings in the subject as a whole, making reference to the attainment target in doing so. Schools are required to keep records on every student, including information on academic achievements, other skills and abilities, and progress in school; how individual schools do this is up to them.

Before too long, (in 2000) 'levels' were introduced on a scale of 1 to 8 so that art and design (along with music) could be seen to be on a par with other subjects with regard to assessment; this, naturally, increased the apparent status of the subject in the eyes of those who value such things. The interesting thing here is that, despite the almost oppressive climate of accountability and monitoring which characterizes contemporary education, teachers are only required by law to assess students' achievement at the end of a key stage (i.e. at ages seven, eleven and fourteen). In practice, of course, most teachers assess their students' performance in art and design far more frequently. The form that such assessment takes can vary widely – from weekly tests to yearly reviews.

Why should teachers assess students' work in art and design?

The general answer to the question 'why assess students' artwork?' is that it provides information. The kind of information gained is dependent upon the nature of the assessment process, as is the value ascribed to it; the needs of the various interested parties will determine both the nature of the assessment and its value. Of these parties, the students themselves have, I would suggest, the greatest interest. They need to know their strengths and weaknesses and what they need to do to improve their practical skills, technical understanding, the quality of their ideas, and their ability to research and realize their intentions. Teachers on the other hand need to judge the effectiveness of their teaching and use this to inform their planning. Other interested parties include the students' parents, who need to know the attainment and progress of their children and need to support their children's learning, and other teachers who need to monitor students' progress across the curriculum and record students' progress and achievement.

Assessment then, in all of its various forms is said to:

- help make clear the teacher's aims and recognizes students' achievement, enabling reflection

- provide feedback to teachers on the effectiveness of their teaching strategies
- help to structure teaching
- provide criteria to support professional judgements
- help ensure that the basic requirements of the syllabus are covered
- support a long-term view of development
- help document progress

It is also said to promote and support students' learning through, for example, discussions arising from group evaluations which can develop students' critical evaluative skills.

These statements appear uncontroversial, but some questions are generated by them, for example: Are there any reasons why we should not assess? Are there potential difficulties or drawbacks of which we should be aware? What is in the best interests of students?

Measurement and accountability, often in their crudest forms, continue to characterize the educational *zeitgeist*. The preferred model for teaching and learning amongst those who effect educational policy continues to be 'objectives' based for the simple reason that it is the most convenient model to ascertain whether a required piece of learning has been taught with efficiency. Elliot Eisner[5] reminds us of the connotations of 'efficiency'

> *Efficiency is largely a virtue for the tasks we don't like to do; few of us like to eat a great meal efficiently or to participate in a wonderful conversation efficiently, or indeed to make love efficiently. What we enjoy the most we linger over. A school system designed with an overriding commitment to efficiency may produce outcomes that have little enduring quality.* (p. xiii)

Enduring qualities, such as those described by Tom Barone in his book *Touching Eternity: The Enduring Outcomes of Teaching*[6], are those outcomes which result from providing students with the opportunity to gain self-esteem through their art-making and by encouraging students to express themselves in their artwork. Barone also highlights how teachers can learn from their students. It is only in a learning environment characterized by mutual respect, where individuals are valued, that meaningful two-way learning can occur. Such dialogue does not militate against the teacher's role as an expert; being an expert or a connoisseur is largely the result of experience and having developed heightened perception, together with the ability to be sensitive to otherwise subliminal characteristics. In the case of art and design, this ability is enhanced by familiarity with the makers' intentions and their development, a familiarity which is often possessed by art and design teachers who engage in a constructive way with their students. In this way I was introduced to the word 'Procrustean' with reference to education; Procrustes is a character from Greek mythology who adjusted travellers' body lengths by stretching them on a rack or chopping off their legs in order to fit his bed. The analogy of course being that a 'one size fits all' approach to education in general and assessment practice in particular is crude and cruel.

Malcolm Ross[7], perhaps the most visible antagonist with regard to assessment in the arts in general, was particularly antagonistic towards examinations, highlighting the following undesirable aspects:

- they are partial – they can only examine the examinable;
- they encourage competition, which can be 'damaging' to artistic endeavour;
- the end product rather than the process is emphasized – therefore experimentation is discouraged;
- they inhibit curriculum innovation;
- they cannot assess 'direct art experience';
- there is undue concentration on 'High Art', as opposed to the vernacular which might be more in tune with the tastes and needs of young people.

Ross summarizes by saying that examination in the arts is not just impracticable but 'altogether undesirable'. Since 1986, when Ross's work was published, things have changed: the notion that 'competition' is an inherently bad thing, seems somewhat naïve, even in the arts. The end product is now considered by many in the profession, including examination boards, to be less important than the process and there is far greater emphasis put upon visual forms other than 'high art'. The partiality of formal assessment processes, such as examinations, however, is perhaps the most important negative trait, and this remains, as does the fact that 'direct art experience' cannot be assessed in any meaningful way. It is also the case that some teachers worry that assessment can introduce elements of judgement or criticism which can inhibit the creative, supportive relationship which is needed with students; there is indeed a tension between support and criticism. In a subject area where personal response is valued highly, there needs to be careful thought as to how give feedback. At its best, assessment in art and design education involves the judgement of a process or a product within a framework of shared values – personal ideas which are shared through negotiation.

Students in schools and colleges are individuals and they have differing individual talents and skills; a truly individualized and learner-centred assessment regime would necessitate the removal of the 'aesthetic' element from the assessment procedure. This would give a fairer and more relevant approach as the focus is then on the students themselves rather than on the work produced (the work being part of the evidence upon which judgements about progress and growth are made).

It is however not the nature of assessment that is the problem, it is the value which is given to it. There is a need to change the 'mindset' with regard to assessment and to demote the status of it. In art and design, this would entail celebrating the essential qualities of aesthetic making and the activities which make art and design teaching worthwhile, including the freedom to fail and the security of knowing that what is personal, idiosyncratic and challenging of convention will not be judged against some remote and impersonal standard of excellence.

Continuous negotiated assessment can facilitate sensitive dialogue; the nature of the subject requires consistent and progressive interplay between teacher and student. This echoes the nature of art-making itself, where making and responding are integrated in the creative process – the painter, for example, often makes a mark – steps back, assesses the result and makes a judgement about the next move. In this way, creating and appraising are inseparable. The reflective appraising dimension may be experienced as a seamless intuitive process, free and spontaneous and tacit.

However, over the past decades, there has been a steady shift in art education away from nurturing young people and facilitating their artistic and aesthetic development; this move has been towards scrutinizing the products of young people's alleged learning in art and design, with an attendant emphasis upon assessment and grading. Consequently, the kind of work which school students are increasingly expected to produce conforms to the requirements of a system which values work which is assessable, and so the partiality of assessment becomes an even more significant issue.

Examinations can have the effect of perpetuating orthodoxies. There is a suspicion that examination boards reward 'safe work', but more troubling is the notion that teaching at the younger age levels is affected by the requirements of examinations. A recent study[8] found little empirical evidence to support either of these claims. However, in an initial pilot study amongst a group of twenty art and design teachers[9], there was a clear indication that the kind of work done at younger age levels was influenced by, if not geared towards, the requirements of public examinations, such as the GCSE.

There is a need to distinguish between assessing the objects which school students produce in their school art lessons from any other kind of made objects. Assessment of art and design in schools is assessment of items which look like art and design objects, but can be seen more as physical evidence of learning. Bearing this in mind, judgement can be more focused and untainted by aesthetic considerations. Art and design teachers are expected to teach young people to know about and understand art and design in its various forms as well as teach them appropriate skills and techniques. Teaching will necessarily entail assessing the extent to which the learners have learned these things, and by implication, the extent to which they as teachers have been successful. To do this, it seems sensible to view the work produced by students in their art and design lessons as evidence of the learning which has taken place. There is a problem with this, of course, and I have noted elsewhere that this perspective has the potential to reduce the whole enterprise to a 'deadening, mechanical and joyless set of activities'[10] which have little to do with things which many associate with aesthetic learning, such as intuition, expression, vision and experimentation – the very things which ought to remain un-assessed. 'Learning', aesthetic or otherwise must be seen to include learning how to enjoy making and learning how to be positively affected towards a range of cultural artefacts if it is to have any real value in an individual's educational life.

John Finney, in writing about assessing what is important in assessing aesthetic learning, comments that 'it is not appropriate to decide in advance what precisely will be learnt'[11]. Finney here is referring to the pervasiveness of the 'objectives' model for teaching, whereby learning is pre-specified and criteria for assessment are linked directly to the stated objectives. In such a model, un-pre-specified worthwhile learning which might materialize from a lesson is inevitably ignored; moreover, the identity of the learner as an individual is subsumed into the larger group. Eleanore Hargreaves, writing in the Cambridge Journal of Education,[12] found that in her sample of secondary schools teachers, the model of assessment employed was overwhelmingly related directly to an objectives-based approach to teaching and learning, an approach uncritically adopted by successive government departments and their agencies. She makes an important observation that the dualities 'summative/formative' and 'of learning/for learning' may not be the most useful way of looking at the issue and that it is more helpful to relate different approaches to assessment to two different conceptions of learning: 'learning-as-attaining-objectives' and 'learning-as-construction-of-knowledge'. I would suggest that the latter is a model which comes most naturally to art and design teachers.

So what is to be done?

If, as I have found, the most important aspects of art-making (at least for many young people and those actively concerned with art-making) are concerned with imagination, intuition, expression, how can these be assessed? Indeed, it does not seem unreasonable to declare that they should not be assessed at all. However, evaluative feedback is necessary, so that students know how well they are doing, but this needs to be negotiated. If criteria are considered to be necessary (to maintain 'standards'?) the community decides on criteria for assessment, but we need to determine the size of the community; I would advocate that the learner's own criteria be used, which means that the community is a minimum of two people; the maximum being whatever practicable number the teacher and learner feel comfortable with. Essentially, the process should be formative and developmentally referenced comparing students' present work with past performance, the whole process being undertaken in a comfortable setting with familiar materials and cultural roles.

The added status which increased formal assessment via examination has given to art, together with a greater emphasis given to cognitive aspects, has been welcomed, for the most part. However, we must ask ourselves whether the enhanced status which is bestowed upon the subject by formal assessment procedures such as public examinations is worth the loss of that which gives the subject its character. Art and design teachers are in a position to make a stand and show the way, after all the Chief Inspector's report of February 05 noted that 'art and design ranks as the best taught National Curriculum subject overall in secondary schools'[13]. I introduced in earlier paragraphs the notion of expertise and intuitive connoisseurship as an important factor in assessing students' work – this is an important element in the whole enterprise. I put forward the phrase 'whippet-fancying' as a positive rather than pejorative term to describe the expertise and tacit knowledge of those art and design educators who can rely on their professional judgement to assess the art and design work of the students in their care with regard to the students themselves rather than with regard to a set of externally imposed criteria. The other vices which I urge teachers of art and design to indulge in are:

- not formally judging and recording students' every classroom activity;
- not pre-specifying outcomes from classroom activities;
- not allowing the assessability of activities to determine their worth.

Students need to be treated as individuals and given a voice. Art and design activities, by their very nature, and especially when the focus is on expression and learning by discovery, facilitate individual learning, the construction of understanding and the development of identity. It follows then that those school art rooms which function well in this respect provide a fertile environment for facilitating creative and mental *growth*, a desirable goal eloquently advocated in Lowenfeld's influential book of the same name.[14]

It is worth reminding ourselves of other 'desirable goals' for art education, as any assessment process needs to be guided by desired outcomes. Aims for art education can be grouped into three broad areas of social utility, visual literacy and personal growth. Of these, personal growth is, by its very nature, of most importance to the individual and it is the individual student who matters. Planning for individualized learning means also planning for differentiated learning. A useful model, used by many teachers, is the simple equation 'some, most, all' (as in 'by the end of the lesson, *some/most/all* students will know, understand or be able to do…'), which can be related to 'working towards, achieving, working beyond'. The problem here is that it is still based on the industrial input-output approach to teaching and learning. Truly differentiated learning is difficult to achieve, but it is facilitated by being based upon an approach to teaching which emphasizes the importance of creating an environment in which learning can *emerge* according to individuals' strengths and aptitudes. If the learning is not pre-specified, then it follows that assessment should be characterized by being developmental, i.e. focusing upon individuals' personal progress, comparing present performance with previous performance. To do this in any meaningful way, it should also be portfolio-based and take the form of a negotiated dialogue between the teacher and the student. Art and design teachers can rely justifiably upon their own instincts, safe in the knowledge that their 'gut reactions' are on a par with fancying whippets, and that is not a bad thing.

Notes and references

1. Eisner, E (2002), *The Arts and the Creation of Mind*, London: Yale University Press.
2. Ross, M (ed.) (1986), *Assessment in Arts Education - A Necessary Discipline or a Loss of Happiness?* Oxford: Pergamon Press.
3. The passages in full are from part VII, written 1st May 1881:

   I have also said that formerly pictures gave me considerable, and music very great delight. But now for many years I cannot endure to read a line of poetry: I have tried lately to read Shakespeare, and found it so intolerably dull that it nauseated me. I have also almost lost my taste for pictures or music. Music generally sets me thinking too energetically on what I have been at work on, instead of giving me pleasure. I retain some taste for fine scenery, but it does not cause me the exquisite delight which it formerly did. […] This curious and lamentable loss of the higher aesthetic tastes is all the odder, as books on history, biographies, and travels (independently of any scientific facts which they may contain), and essays on all sorts of subjects interest me as much as ever they did. My mind seems to have become a kind of machine for grinding general laws out of large collections of facts, but why this should have caused the atrophy of that part of the brain alone, on which the higher tastes depend, I cannot conceive. A man with a mind more highly organised or better constituted than mine, would not, I suppose, have thus suffered; and if I had to live my life again, I would have made a rule to read some poetry and listen to some music at least once every week; for perhaps the parts of my brain now atrophied would thus have been kept active through use. The loss of these tastes is a loss of happiness, and may possibly be injurious to the intellect, and more probably to the moral character, by enfeebling the emotional part of our nature.

   From Barlow, N (ed.) (1969), *The autobiography of Charles Darwin, 1809–1882: with original omissions restored*, New York: W.W. Norton.

4. The attainment target for art & design is simply 'Knowledge, Skills and Understanding'; teachers are expected to identify the aspects of art and design in which pupils make progress in the following four aspects of this attainment target:

   - *exploring and developing ideas*
   - *investigating and making art, craft and design*
   - *evaluating and developing work*
   - *developing knowledge and understanding*

5. Eisner, E *op. cit.*
6. Barone, T (2001), *Touching Eternity: The Enduring Outcomes of Teaching*, New York: Teachers College Press.
7. Ross, M. (1986), Against Assessment, in *Assessment in Arts Education*, Oxford: Pergamon.
8. Mason, R, Steers, J, Bedford, D and McCabe, C (2005), *The impact of formal assessment on secondary school art and design education: A systematic description of empirical studies*, EPPI centre, London. See http:// eppi.ioe.ac.uk.
9. This was in the form of a questionnaire, the first question of which was: Does formal assessment of art & design at Key Stage 4 and beyond have an impact upon the nature and content of the subject at Key Stage 3? The results in full can be obtained from the author.
10. Hickman, R (2005), *Why We Make Art - and why it is taught*, Bristol: Intellect.
11. Finney, J (2002), Assessing what is important, in *Name – The national association of music educators magazine*, (2) 9, p.9.
12. Hargreaves, E (2005), Assessment for learning? Thinking outside the (black) box, in *Cambridge Journal of Education* 35 (2), pp. 213–224.
13. Bell, D *The Annual Report of Her Majesty's Chief Inspector of Schools 2003/4*, London: DfES (Ofsted).
14. Lowenfeld, V (1947), *Creative and Mental Growth*, New York: Macmillan.

Bibliography

Allison, B (1986), 'Some Aspects of Assessment in Art & Design', in M. Ross (ed.), *Assessment in Arts Education – A Necessary Discipline or a Loss of Happiness?* Oxford: Pergamon Press.

Ash, A Schofield, K and Starkey, A (2000), Assessment and Examinations in Art & Design, in L Burgess and N Addison (eds.), *Learning to Teach Art & Design in the Secondary School*, London: RoutledgeFalmer.

Aspin, D (1981), Assessment & Education in the Arts, in M Ross (ed.), *The Aesthetic Imperative*, Oxford: Pergamon.

Aspin, D (1986), Objectivity and Assessment in the Arts: the problem of Aesthetic Education, in M Ross (ed.), *Assessment in Arts Education*, Oxford: Pergamon.

Barrett, M (1982), *Art Education*, London: Heinemann.

Best, D (1992), *The Rationality of Feeling*, Lewes: Falmer Press.

Boughton, D, Eisner, E and Ligtvoet (eds.) (1996), *Evaluating and Assessing the Visual Arts*, New York: Teachers College Press.

Day, M D (1985), Evaluating Student Achievement in Discipline-based Art Programs, *Studies in Art Education*, 26 (4) 232–240.

Eisner, E (1963), Evaluating Children's Art, in G Pappas (ed.) (1970), *Concepts in Art and Education*, London: Collier-Macmillan.
Eisner, E (1971), How Can You Measure A Rainbow? Tactics for Evaluating the Teaching of Art, in *Art Education*, vol. 24, no. 5, NAEA.
Kennedy, M (1995), Approaching Assessment, in R Prentice (ed.), *Teaching Art and Design*, London: Cassell.

Chapter 8: Towards a more complex description of the role of assessment as a practice for nurturing strategic intelligence in art education

Leslie Cunliffe

Introduction

Some of the issues that have to be resolved if dispositions for self-regulated learning are to be nurtured in art education during key stage 2 (age 7-11) and more firmly cultivated at key stage 3 (age 11-14) and beyond, can be easily grasped by reporting two recent conversations. The first conversation was between a colleague and a head of art from a local secondary school. The colleague was interested to know whether the teacher in question could identify the reasons why GCSE art results in an alternative school had improved. (The General Certificate in Secondary Education is a public examination taken by sixteen-year-olds, with sixty per cent of the final mark awarded for coursework done any time during the previous two years.) The teacher attributed the better results to students engaging in more reviewing and modifying of their work. The colleague then made the suggestion that if this strategy improved GCSE results, it might be significant for improving learning at key stage 3, which, in turn, would have further, strategic impact on learning from the age of fourteen onwards. The art teacher in question rejected this suggestion on the grounds that there was not enough time at key stage 3 for students to engage in reviewing and modifying their work. Here we have an example of an experienced art teacher identifying the factors that lead to a big improvement in learning and progression at key stage 4 in one school, only to then deny its general significance for improving learning and progression at key stage 3 and beyond in her own school. The second conversation was between a head of art and an art advisor that was overheard by a PGCE art student. The head of art said to the advisor that having his students review and modify their art was a waste of time as he had tried it for a month and got nowhere. The fallacy in this remark is to think that developing the good habits of mind for productively engaging in self-regulated learning is something that can be achieved in a month, which of course is not a viewpoint shared by those who promote the educational significance of meta-cognition. Both the art teachers above fail to grasp why meta-cognition is being given increasing attention in mainstream education in the UK, and why it is considered to be the jewel in the crown in both the older thinking skills approach to education as well as the more recent dispositional, sociocultural paradigm of learning.[1]

Meta-cognition

Meta-cognition describes the operation of the mind at a 'meta-level', that is, beyond normal cognition. The word itself was first used in a Ph.D. thesis completed by Hart at Stanford University in 1965.[2] Gombrich's[3] analysis of artistic processes as engaging with 'schema and correction', originally given as the A. W. Mellon Lectures in Washington in1956, anticipates this general growing interest in meta-cognition, as the *correction* part of

Gombrich's dialectical method is another way of describing the feedback process.[4] The schema part of Gombrich's method equates with using cognitive strategies and cognitive resources that are needed for generating art, which is always achieved by individuals or groups appropriating the necessary habits of mind, deposit of competencies or skills, insights about style, choice of subject matter, and wider purposes that provide a direction for making art that emerges from the culture. The cognitive strategies that give corrective feedback to the deployment of the schemas for generating art are also acquired from the culture. Gombrich believed that the greatest artists are those who have the most sophisticated forms of meta-cognition.[5]

There is a growing body of literature in psychology and educational research on the subject of meta-cognition, which is belatedly shaping educational policy and practice.

In art education, meta-cognition was officially introduced through the National Curriculum's requirement that students should be taught how to evaluate and develop their work. The introduction of meta-cognition in the generically taught key skills for the fourteen to sixteen and the sixteen to nineteen phases of education is another sign of its perceived importance for improving educational practice for the twenty-first century. More recently, following on from the National Curriculum, meta-cognition has been embedded in both the GCSE and post-16 art assessment objectives, and can be found in the generic requirements of the key stage 3 strategy that was introduced into secondary education in the UK in 2002 to include, amongst others, a strand related to thinking skills and one involving assessment for learning.

The thinking skills strand of the key stage 3 strategy requires pupils across the curriculum to constantly and deliberately rehearse their ability to identify problems, create ideas, plan for and try options, and apply methods to solutions. The assessment for learning strand requires pupils across the curriculum to constantly and conscientiously create and meet targets, review work, and identify strengths and weaknesses in achievement. The forms of cognition described under the thinking skills strands of the key stage 3 strategy are generally known in the research literature as strategies for planning and generating, with those listed under the assessment for learning strand known as cognitive processes for monitoring and checking (see **Figure 1**).[6]

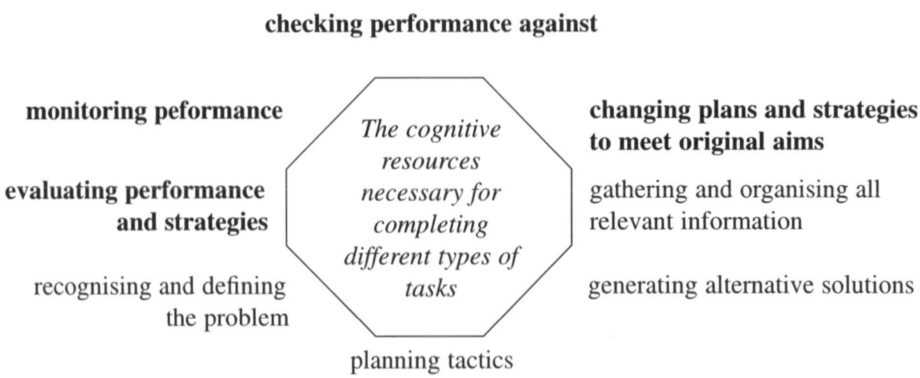

Figure 1: Cognitive strategies: four for planning and generating; four for monitoring and checking [in bold]

Both types of cognitive strategies can be distinguished from cognitive resources, the acquisition of which has been the traditional purpose of education. These are the cognitive tools like language, knowledge and skills that need to be acquired in order to function properly in any given educational or other context, in that they involve the skills that are basic to any performance. In art, one such cognitive resource would be to know how to load a brush with the right amount of paint to achieve a desired result. Another might be related to acquiring language and concepts to know, say, some of the cultural factors that determine traditional tribal practices of Australian Aboriginal art. The former cognitive resource is for a procedural or a 'know how' category of knowledge. The latter form of cognitive resource is for a 'know that' form of declarative knowledge. The role of cognitive and meta-cognitive strategies involve monitoring how best to deploy such cognitive resources, as it would be useless to have a fine set of tools without knowing how to use them properly, or to have to rely on others to give directions each time someone wanted to use them correctly.

The significance of meta-cognition for improving educational and creative performance can be gleaned from **Table 1**,[7] which summarizes research into the salient features of the cognitive processes, dispositions and character traits that need to be in place if students are to regulate their own learning and creative potential. This is the capacity to reproduce culture through engaging with the process of enculturation, and the way this facilitates the process of transformation of mind in culture. Column four bridges column one, two and three with column five, in that it specifies the cognitive processes, character traits and cognitive resources that are needed for both reproducing culture and for achieving cultural transformation. Column six specifies the dispositions and character traits that the teacher has to mediate and foster if students are to regulate their own creativity.

The table is also useful for understanding the move from a view of mind promoted in the older paradigm of cognitive psychology as analogous with the way computers process information, towards a social or discursive view of mind that engages the motivation to want to think and act in certain ways, which, of course, is not an attribute that human beings share with computers. This would account for why motivation and engagement is another strand in the key stage 3 strategy.

It follows from this analysis that developing and improving students' abilities and desires to use cognitive and meta-cognitive strategies and the related character traits should be the rationale for all assessment or feedback processes in art education. A corollary of such an approach would be to inaugurate a change from teachers being responsible for the summative assessment of students' work towards having them take responsibility for evaluating their students' capacities to diagnose the strengths and weaknesses of their own performance, as the former, current approach might simply indicate results obtained by teaching for the summative outcome. Parsons makes the same point when he states: 'It seems to me unlikely that one can tell by looking at studio work whether a student has understood a particular concept or has blindly followed the teacher's suggestion'.[8]

Each of the cognitive processes, dispositions and character traits in **Table 1** has to be used in conjunction with the others. For example, a student's capacity to work independently must be evaluated against the way this successfully engages other dispositions as independence,

1. Commonly listed strategies needed for self-regulated learning (from Inset & Shuck Smith 1986)	2. Cognitive strategies needed for self-regulated learning (from Blagg 1993)	3. Dispositions needed to be cultivated for self-regulated learning (from Jay, Perkins & Tishman 1993)	4. Cognitive aspects that need to be cultivated for self-regulated creativity (from Cropley 1997)	5. Dispositions and character traits needed to be cultivated for self-regulated creativity (from Cropley 1997)	6. Dispositions and character traits that teachers have to foster to support the development of self-regulated creativity (from Cropley 1997)
Asking questions: defining hypotheses, establishing aims, discovering audience, relating task to previous work, etc	Gathering and organising all relevant information	To be broad and adventurous	Possession of a fund of general knowledge	To ability to be curious, adventurous, and a tolerance for ambiguity	Encourage students to learn independently
Planning: deciding on tactics and timetables, reduction of task or problem into components: what physical or mental skills are necessary?	Recognising and defining the problem and planning tactics	To plan a course of action and be strategic	Knowledge of one or more special fields	The ability to show task commitment, persistence, and determination by deliberately practising the necessary skills and knowledge	Have a cooperative, socially integrated style of teaching
Monitoring: continuous attempt to match efforts, answers and discoveries to initial questions or purpose	Generating alternative solutions	To clarify and seek understanding	An active imagination	The ability to be independent	Take students' suggestions and questions seriously
Checking: preliminary assessment of performance and results	Checking performance against original aims	To sustain intellectual curiosity	Ability to recognise, discover, or invent problems	Having self-confidence and the willingness to risk being wrong	Encourage flexible thinking in students
Revising: may be simple re-drafting or re-calculation or may involve setting of revised goals	Evaluating performance and strategies	To be intellectually careful	Skill at seeing connections, overlaps, similarities, and logical implications (convergent thinking)	The drive to experiment and the willingness to try difficult tasks	Help students to learn to cope with frustration and failure, so that they have the courage to try the new and unusual
Self-Testing: final self-assessment both of results and performance on task	Monitoring performance and revising plans and strategies to meet original aims	To be meta-cognitive	Ability and willingness to evaluate their own work		Promote self-evaluation in students
	Gathering and organising all relevant information	To seek and evaluate reasons	Ability to think up many ways to solve problems		Offer students opportunities to work with a wide variety of materials and under different conditions
	Changing plans and strategies to meet original aims		Skill at making remote associations, bisociating, accepting primary process material, forming new gestalts, etc. (divergent thinking)		
			A preference for accommodating rather than assimilating		
			Ability to communicate their own results to other people		

Table 1: Recent research findings that identify the cognitive processes, dispositions and traits needed for developing self-regulated capacities for creative performance predicated on higher order thinking (apart from column 4, the skills or cognitive resources necessary for such a performance are assumed rather made explicit in this table).

in itself, does not guarantee quality in learning. Collating these variables is a very demanding exercise that can only be achieved through planning for self-regulated learning in a strategic way, and is a reason why, unlike mathematical whiz kids, there are no exceptionally creative artistic whiz kids on the block, as the successful collation of the relevant skills, knowledge, dispositions, cognitive processes and traits needed for an exceptional creative performance requires wisdom to know how to deploy the relevant heuristics, in contrast to being able to reliably apply, say, algorithmic rules for mathematics.[9]

In this respect, assessment for learning how to learn relocates normative properties away from the teacher making judgements about temporary acts or mindsets, in favour of cultivating the stable dispositions, character traits and reliable cognitive processes that enable students' to accurately form judgements about their own learning, so that what is considered normative is agent-based as opposed to act- or belief-based, as actions and beliefs are finally justified through the character traits of agents as opposed to some external source of validity. To take this form of analysis beyond its potentially dualistic structure of agent- or act-based, we can draw on Aristotle's[10] idea of cultivating and practising virtue as an agent-focused process, which is summarized very well by Nietzsche as 'a long obedience in the same direction'. This has the advantage of making the causal link between an agent's motives and the same agent's right acts and correct beliefs normative for the practice of art education. In other words, it is the student's capacity to accurately diagnose the strengths and weaknesses in their own work that should be seen as normative for assessment, which is as much an ethical as epistemic issue as the judgements require honesty and integrity, if they are to be cognitively reliable.

Neglecting the importance of ethics for optimizing the cognitive processes for thinking and creativity is a deficiency of all the lists in **Table 1**. A reason why students find meta-cognition difficult is that reflection is an ethically demanding process. A corollary of this is that a person who has developed cognitively reliable habits of mind could use these for unethical ends. Equally, high levels of creativity can serve unethical purposes. Therefore ethical norms should be included when developing any heuristics for reproducing and transforming culture, as thinking is always an ethical as well as an epistemic and creative issue.[11]

The current situation

The assessment of achievement in art education currently serves a variety of purposes, with the related data providing information for government, local authorities, schools, teachers, further and higher education institutions, future employers, parents and students. All of these purposes for assessment are in place as a way of informing the various stakeholders in the educational process; however, the one function least catered for in current practice is the role of assessment for enabling students to learn how to regulate their own learning.

This issue of learning how to learn is at the centre of recent educational debate about the purposes of assessment, as research[12] shows that certain methods of assessment are more likely to improve performance because they focus on nurturing dispositions for meta-cognition rather than being predicated on teaching for the test, teaching for the result in coursework, or teacher-led short-term approaches for engaging with so-called radical creativity. In other words, assessment practices and teaching strategies that are teaching focused are least likely to lead to students knowing how to regulate their own learning.

Ofsted reports on assessment practices in secondary art education

The inability of the two teachers to appreciate the importance of nurturing strategic meta-cognitive dispositions discussed in the introduction is widespread, and might be the reason why the development of forms of assessment for systematically and strategically planning to improve students' capacity to regulate their own learning continues to be neglected in art education. This judgement is based on a succession of Ofsted inspection reports[13] for secondary art education, although it is recognized that Ofsted's collection and use of data does not comply with approved research methods. Nevertheless, the data need to be taken into account given that it provides the only current source about what is going on in a large number of secondary school art departments.

Although Ofsted reports rarely discuss the ability of students to independently review and modify their work, which in itself is illuminating, the picture the reports paint of more basic assessment practices in art education is unflattering, especially those related to teachers practising meta-cognition in their teaching. The 1997-1998 **Ofsted Summary Report of Secondary Art Inspections** paints a poor picture of assessment practices in art at key stage 3, with only one-third of inspected departments being judged to have good practice. It goes on to state that fewer than one-third of the art departments that were inspected used assessment data to help evaluate and review the quality of teaching and learning. Given that this is the case, the report's finding that good progress is made by a little less than half of schools at key stage 3 is surprising; it would be expected to be lower given the previously stated statistics. The report also contrasts the relatively weak practice of assessment at key stage 3 with that at GCSE and post-16, where the assessment procedures and assessment objectives of external examinations have made more impact on the rigour of assessment methods used by teachers.

Although the 2000-2001 **Ofsted Report on Art and Design Inspections** identifies improvements on the previously low baseline of assessment practices described for 1997-1998, it also states that 'the quality of assessment remains variable, with inadequacies in assessment procedures in one in ten schools and the use of assessment information in one in five schools'. The report goes on to describe how assessment data is still not being effectively used to improve teaching and learning: 'Inadequacies in the monitoring, evaluation and development of teaching in the subject also persist, with nearly one in five schools displaying weak practice'. Ofsted's concern about such poor assessment practices might explain the motivation to publish **Good Assessment Practices in Art and Design** in 2003, which attempted to specify better approaches, while at the same time neglecting to give sustained treatment to the importance of meta-cognition for cultivating independent learning in art.

In the Ofsted **Art Subject Report** for 2003/2004 there is no specific discussion of assessment; however, a discerning reader can identify how inadequate approaches to assessment underpin many of the problems highlighted in the report, especially the important role of meta-cognition for developing learning dispositions that have strategic educational value. For example, the report mentions that the key stage 3 strategy, which I have already described as addressing thinking skills, assessment for learning and motivation and engagement, 'appears to have passed the subject by'. Furthermore, the report highlights the episodic and fragmented nature of a lot of art curricula and learning, which results in handicapping progress from one key stage or phase of education to the next, or one art teacher to the next, and with it the associated ability to plan learning in a deliberate, strategic or future-tense way.[14]

The background to past and current misconceptions about assessment in art education

The picture painted in Ofsted inspection reports reflects attitudes and misconceptions about assessment in art education that can be traced to their genesis in the romantic and modernist paradigm of art education. With the romantic and modernist paradigm, the process of assessment is perceived as an imposition of arbitrary values and standards that inhibit or destroy self-expression, creativity and learning. The argument is an extension of the view that because each person is innately creative, expressive and unique, formulating normative assessment criteria is both impossible and destructive.[15] With the romantic conception of art education, the student or person is represented as an isolated natural object rather than a sociocultural artefact,[16] making any social and cultural influence, including the feedback systems that tradition has developed for improving artwork, unhelpful for the natural, uninhibited and intuitive flow of self-expression and creativity.

The romantic and modernist view of assessment as inimical to creativity and learning was reinforced by the parallel development in the proliferation of styles in modernist practices of art. These more individual styles of art seemingly undermined the validity of assessing one version of art against any other, as is the practice with norm-referenced assessment. In some respects, the hostility against assessment found in the romantic, modernist paradigm of art education was justified, if this is understood as an implicit critique of norm-referenced, summative and impressionistic methods of assessment, which are arbitrary and authoritarian. That such methods persist in many assessment practices in schools, where teachers continue to ignore the importance of using shared criteria, preferring instead to assess work from a god-like perspective, is best understood as a legacy of modernist practice. Such practices are also common in higher education. Mitchell[17] exposed the problems that students encounter when assessment is carried out from the god-like perspective, where lecturers intuitively and impressionistically read motives and values into students' work that result in 'discourse being riven with conflict', so that 'to award a student an average class of degree is to fly in the face of the 'achievement of uniqueness', where uniqueness is not communicated as the product of successful orientation, but rather as free-floating subjectivity'.[18]

This approach to assessment is a reflection of the art educator's metaphysical stance, which in turn is a mirror image of the modernist self-expressive stance. From such a god-like position, all-knowing judgements can be made without fear of contradiction or due consideration being given to the complexity of the cognitive processes in relationship to how both procedural and declarative forms of knowledge have been used, and the criteria and other values students have drawn on to inform the working process. Because lecturers still operate with idiosyncratic and secret criteria, by definition, this cannot be mediated to their students. It goes without saying that such an approach to assessment does little or nothing to nurture and promote students' meta-cognition and, therefore, should not be confused with assessment practices that will be advocated in this chapter.

A wider legacy of thought that perpetuates the opposite fallacy to that of the intuitive approach to assessment discussed above is to believe that only quantitative assessment methods are valid. The bias for quantitative methods of assessment reflects wider historical trends in enlightenment and modern thought that systematically privileged the first of the following concepts over the second in these dualisms: objective/subjective, rational/irrational, certainty/ambiguity, outer/inner, quantitative/qualitative, secondary process thinking/primary process thinking, declarative knowledge/procedural knowledge, mind/body, left-brain hemisphere functions/right-brain hemisphere functions, tuition/intuition, analytical/creative, cultural/natural, reproducing culture/transforming culture. (It should be noted that the presentation of such dichotomies does not indicate their validity, as the purpose in recording them is to engage in a diagnostic activity aimed at exposing this type of thinking.) The modernist paradigm of art education has persistently played out a false and futile contest by polemically affirming the second category of concepts in reaction to the first category. In so doing, it becomes impaled on the problems generated by the dualistic analysis rather than going beyond the problems by providing a solution.

Such a false contest informs Curtis'[19] discussion of assessment in art education, in which he argues for a more active engagement with intuition to 'take into account qualities which go beyond what is immediately apparent'. Wittgenstein[20] denied such a shadow mentalist world of thinking that supposedly lies behind the real world of experience and action. For Curtis' occult-like intuition to operate in a normative way in assessment, both within a community of practice of art educators and with novices like students who work on the edge of such a practice, the intuitive judgements would need to flow from following rules that have been explicitly formulated and agreed for actions. The unconscious processes or habits of mind that inform authentic expert performance result from following such rules, which are very different from the way novices operate by acting in accordance with the rules. I know from experiencing assessment within a so-called community of practice that one person's intuitive or impressionistic evaluation of art is best understood not by invoking such occult-like mental states but by seeing the practice as resulting from the sociocultural perspective of an out-of-date conception of assessment. For example, when GCSE examiners fail to read the written evidence submitted in sketchbooks and other sources, are they operating with intuition or are they unaware of the significance of declarative knowledge for engaging with the assessment of knowledge and understanding of art in its social and cultural context?[21]

In identifying intuition as an important but neglected component for assessing art, Curtis makes the mistake of not distinguishing, as Wittgenstein did, between cases of rule following that are explicitly formulated for actions, and cases where people comply with rules by acting in accordance with them. For intuition to become normative in the practice of assessment, the intuitive judgements would have to be consistent with the first example of rule following in which rules are explicitly formulated for managing actions. Rom Harré makes this telling point about rule following:

> *We can say that a rule is* ***immanent*** *in a practice if the normative character of what is being done comes from simply learning the practice, but a rule could be formulated to express the normative character of the practice. In contrast, a rule is* ***transcendent*** *to a practice if the rule exists in the same symbolic realm as the practice, such as when an actor attends to a rule and uses it as an instruction for performing certain actions, or a teacher deploys a rule to guide the actions of a pupil. A rule may be* ***transcendent*** *to the practice for the trainer but immanent for the learner, if the latter is not taught the practice by being given the rule as an instruction.*[22]

Curtis' attempt to promote the role of intuition in assessment reveals a preoccupation with the metaphysical stance of the modernist art educator rather than any concern to articulate a sociocultural practice of assessment that aims to nurture students' dispositions to monitor their own performance, which would be a good example of the significance of how Wittgenstein's notion of explicitly formulating rules for action is carried out in practice. GCSE assessment objectives, for example, are formulated to enable students to increasingly manage the normative character for their own actions, with the view to eventually operating at a meta-level to monitor such actions, a case of having learned how to learn how to provide the appropriate evidence to meet GCSE criteria.

Curtis' discussion of assessment can be seen as a misguided reaction to the broader cultural pressures that attempt to reduce all forms of knowledge to scientific or quantitative analysis, which has resulted in making a religion out of science known as scientism but which in fact has nothing to do with the practice of science. This is at the root of the prevalence of the continued use of dualisms like 'objective' and 'subjective' in discussions of assessment in art education, which only serves the purpose of perpetuating the existing sickness of thought by obfuscating the way judgements emerge from a sociocultural reality of a community of practice and its related established criteria and values. As Best has pointed out, all approaches to assessment, including quantification, require such judgements:

> *Assessment in the arts, as in many spheres, is necessarily a matter of judgment. It is a confusion to assume that only quantification, and not judgment, can give genuinely objective assessment, since the meaning of the quantification requires judgment.*[23]

As judgement underpins all good assessment practices, it is wrong to argue that it is either inappropriate to use well-formulated, explicit criteria to inform assessment in a subject like art because it is supposedly not reducible to such criteria, or to argue that authenticity in assessing art means engaging with occult-like intuition, as judgements in assessment have to be determined by the application of explicitly formulated rules built on professional and communal standards. On occasions, the criteria for the judgements might lack the fine-grained features to match all the qualities present in some of the artwork for which it has been formulated, but this should not be a source of concern as such limitations are normative for all practices and disciplines, as the world is always more fine-grained than any version by which we can evaluate or understand it. However, this does not mean that the versions we create do not have fitness for purpose or give real knowledge or be good instruments for practice.

A corollary of relying on dualistic discourse to frame objections to normative criteria in assessment results in art educators continuing to uncritically and unjustifiably stress or dichotomize dispositions like risk-taking and playfulness over against other dispositions that are also critical for nurturing self-regulated learning and creativity. No doubt this is why Jay, Perkins & Tishman[24] see the ability to be broad and adventurous as needing to be deployed with other dispositions like 'the ability to sustain intellectual curiosity, to clarify and seek understanding, to plan a course of action and be strategic, to be intellectually careful, to seek and evaluate reasons, and to be meta-cognitive'. See column 3 in **Table 1**.

The deep irony of such an emphasis on risk-taking is that it fails to make any sense of the complexity of the background conditions that allow students to take self-directed risks. If voluntarily breaking a rule is a logical extension of knowing how to follow a rule, a condition that is radically different from breaking a rule through ignorance, then risk-taking must be a corollary of risk assessment. The research shows that taking potentially profitable as opposed to deleterious risks or being risk aversive is the result of appropriating and deploying sophisticated knowledge and self-regulated patterns of thought.[25] The apparent improvisational nature of productive risk-taking only appears so because it is structured by previously learned, regulated thinking. No doubt Charlie Parker took risks in developing the bebop genre of jazz; however, Owens[26] attributes Parker's ability to take such creative risks to his appropriation of a vast range of 'formulaic' jazz music. It turns out that being able to take risks in jazz improvisation results from a background, extensive knowledge of jazz, an account that is consistent with Gombrich's[27] earlier analysis of this process in visual art as 'formula and experience'. Productive risk-taking is not improvised in a cultural vacuum, as any fool can impulsively take misguided risks.

The singular emphasis on risk-taking that occasionally breaks out like a virus in the art education literature[28] is marked by the same modernist metaphysical stance as that occupied by the intuitive art educator discussed above, in that both neglect the background, sociocultural conditions that would make it possible for students to both flourish at taking independent risks and to regulate their own learning.

A review of the literature[29] reveals the discussion of assessment in art education that is usually framed in a culturally specific, historical or principled way but without regard to how such principles can be more firmly grounded by empirical evidence to ascertain better classroom practice for improving learning in the subject. One such discussion is by Ash, Schofield and Starkey,[30] who describe the basic differences in formative, summative and ipsative forms of assessment. Within formative assessment they discriminate between its informal use by the teacher as a way of giving continuous feedback to guide and encourage pupils about their performance on an activity, a practice known as ipsative assessment, and the more deliberate formative practice of self-assessment that develops and improves a student's ability to diagnose their own strengths and weaknesses, so they can go on to eventually learn how to learn. The former method of practising formative assessment equates with a teacher-to-pupil emphasis or direction of fit, and the latter as a learner-to-teacher direction of fit, a contrast between the teacher being in control of the judgements that inform the feedback process, and the pupil learning how to take control of their own learning. Boekaerts[31] describes the latter as self-regulated learning. Zimmerman & Schunk describe self-regulated learning as 'self-generated thoughts, feelings, and actions, which are systematically orientated toward attainment of students' own goals'.[32]

Ash, Schofield and Starkey fail to make enough of a distinction between assessment practices that are teacher-regulated as opposed to those that aim to develop self-regulated learning. For example, an art teacher's ongoing, informal feedback does not necessarily result in students acquiring the dispositions for engaging with self-regulated learning. On balance, this type of informal feedback is just as likely to result in passive learning, in which the student successfully follows the advice given by the teacher but without knowing or understanding why they are doing what they are doing, as would be the case with self-regulated learning. Teaching styles that lead to passive or surface learning in art are far more widespread than is generally thought, and can be easily disguised by the conjuring trick of achieving the best GCSE or A level results in the school, now commonly referred to as, say, seventy-five per cent A-C's of 'good results', an attitude of mind that is the same as teaching for the test. In contrast, self-regulated learning gives priority to cultivating the dispositions and virtues that would enable students to genuinely learn how to learn, which might equate with, say, only thirty-two per cent of students currently achieving self-regulated learning, which would be a far better indication of a genuine educational outcome than the so-called good results referred to above.

Learning theory and assessment practices

Desforges[33] highlights four areas of research into learning that can inform the practice of assessment. The research ranges form causal factors related to neural mechanisms all the way through to the operation of mind in expert performance, the distributed mind of a community of practice found in participation theory, to the more dispersed view of mind that activity theory explores. The four areas of research can be seen as analogous to a Russian doll, with the neural mind represented by the smallest doll, followed by expert performance, participation theory, leaving activity theory to be represented by the largest doll. Because learning is complex, any attempt to specify the sociocultural conditions for improving self-regulated learning through assessment will need this multi-level analysis.

Learning and neural science

The general implications of research into neural mechanisms highlights the importance of being trained to act in accordance with a rule. Harré puts it like this:

> *In training people we create in them artificial neural mechanisms. In this way habits partake of the causal. But in that their origin is cultural and their assessment overt, they partake of the monitored.*[34]

In this account, the ingrained and habitual, that is, cultural, become indistinguishable from the inborn and causal, that is, genetic. That such neural mechanisms are the product of well-learned routines does not in any way deny their capacity to operate in flexible and adaptive ways.[35] Strauss & Quinn describe this process in the following passage.

> *They (schemas) can adapt to new or ambiguous situations with 'regulated improvisation,' to use Bourdieu's term (1977, p.11). The reactions...are improvisational because they are created on the spot, but regulated because they are guided by previously learned patterns of associations, they are not improvised out of thin air.*[36]

Research in neural science gives a causal turn to Aristotle's idea that achieving excellence is the product of acquiring good and reliable habits of mind that go down deep, thus reinforcing the need for students to deliberately rehearse meta-cognition in a sustained way, so that their neural networks are literally changed, over time, by such a practice.

Learning and expert performance

The causal chain in becoming an expert involves introductory exploration, getting the idea, and practice to sufficiency for creating automatic cognitive routines. Arrested development occurs when there is a breakdown in one or more of these links. Becoming an expert involves a continuous process of setting new goals, designing new ways of advancing such goals and thus avoiding arrested development, all of which require continuous monitoring of the situation to include deliberate planning in preparation and evaluation and deliberate planning for flexibility.

How people achieve expertise and go about their tasks is significant for determining classroom practices to improve self-regulated learning because experts implicitly use and model the dispositions that novices need to explicitly cultivate and deploy. There is a steady growth of literature on expert performance, which has identified the critical importance of what is known as the ten-year rule. This is the time needed to deliberately and intensively learn and practice a discipline that has been identified in research across many disciplines. Mozart and Picasso, who started very early in their chosen fields, and who were endowed with the necessary cognitive faculties and supportive social circumstances to accelerate their creative development, conform to the ten-year model, as they only began to make original art of lasting worth after the ten-year period had elapsed.[37] Howe[38] draws on empirical evidence to show that achieving expertise also requires the ten-year rule of deliberate practice to be combined with the rule of expert instruction.

Learning and participation theory

The participation theory of learning[39] shifts the unit of analysis away from an expert performer's individual mind to the way individual minds are embedded in communities of practice that provide expert instruction. Participation theory situates such learning in mentor/apprenticeship relationships, which broadly equates with the process of enculturation by example. Black and Wiliam,[40] describe this process in relationship to learning when students are 'apprenticed into a guild' in the practice of peer- and self-assessment by learning how to use specific criteria to evaluate their work.

The participation theory of learning is consonant with new research into creativity.[41] Weisberg[42] discusses the important role mentors play in the process of someone achieving excellence in creativity. Kroeber[43] highlights the significance of good role models for imparting knowledge, as they provide examples that can be imitated, while also acting as pacemakers who set and maintain high standards. McClelland[44] describes how in a variety of cultures positive attitudes towards achievement is promoted through good role models, or through narratives of past exemplars told to the young. Simonton[45] correlated high levels of creativity in a current generation with the endeavours of the two previous generations. Ochse's[46] argument for a more positive view of the role of secondary process thinking for realizing excellence in creativity fits with participation theory, in that deliberate learning requires certain social and cultural factors to be in place if individuals are to flourish in a community of practice. Such richer descriptions of the process of creativity reflect a shift away from the individual as the unit of analysis towards a sociocultural understanding of individual achievement, so that 'the phenomenon of creativity…is as much a cultural and social as it is a psychological event'.[47]

Learning and activity theory

Activity theory[48] is a systemic approach to learning and creativity to include participation theory, expert performance and neural mechanisms that have their origins in the culture, so that the 'activity system' of the entire extended community and the wider environment becomes the unit of analysis rather than just the community of practice or an individual mind. While activity theory does justice to the multidimensional complexity of learning and creativity in human culture, this strength is also its weakness because it makes the theory difficult to test in empirical research.[49] Activity theory wrestles with identifying the relationship between the causal factors that determine an individual's capacity to reproduce culture (the process of enculturation) and the way this engages with or relates to wider external cultural transformation (the process of transformation of mind in culture).

The wider research context of assessment for learning

The shortfall in assessment practices to meet the desirable aim of mapping progression and developing strategic learning identified earlier in this chapter by citing, amongst other things, Ofsted art subject reports broadly converges with evidence from wider educational research into the relationship between assessment practices, learning and progression. Over the last decade, Black & Wiliam[50] have developed a paradigm for good assessment that they hope will improve learning. It is based on surveying two hundred and fifty research papers. Below is a summary of the shortcomings in assessment practices that emerged from their review of the research literature:

- Although much current teaching is done in a conscientious way, the form in which it is carried out has the tendency to short-circuit the development of the meta-cognitive dispositions that result in students engaging in deeper learning.
- Teaching methods are not openly discussed, shared or peer reviewed, with inadequate attention given to colleagues' previous assessment records of the learning and progression of pupils.
- The wide range of work that is undertaken with pupils, by its very nature, often sabotages the quality of learning that it is supposed to generate. A related problem occurs when the management of the assessment process results in giving marks at the expense of providing more fruitful, qualitative feedback, as this seems to be the vital ingredient in improving learning by assessment practices.
- Too much emphasis on external testing motivates teachers to fine-tune their ability to teach for the test rather than to focus on diagnosing pupils' real learning needs.
- Summative assessment carried out at the end of a unit of work serves no learning purpose because by then it is too late for pupils to act in a formative way on the assessment feedback to improve their learning on that unit of work, although such summative feedback might have an effect on the next unit of work if this is similar to the previous one.
- When assessment primarily serves the purpose of providing information for government, higher education, future employers and other external bodies, it can easily conflict with the more desirable aim of enabling pupils to learn how to learn.
- When attainment is recorded using easily digested methods like norm-referencing, or when grades are given without the accompanying supplementary diagnostic comments and processes, this has a deleterious effect on learning. The less able become apathetic because they wrongly confuse or associate grades with their 'real' ability, a consequence of which is that such pupils learn to avoid complex tasks as these are construed as confirming their low position in the class. The effect is equally damaging on more able pupils who lose sight of what really matters in the learning process because they concentrate their attention on superficial or surface approaches to learning aimed at getting the right result rather than engaging the full range of dispositions that are required for learning how to learn.

Black & Wiliam see self-regulated learning as the key for overcoming the shortcomings identified above, which, in turn, might establish the conditions by which students can both re-create and transform culture. This is a summary of their recommendations:

- The problem of low attainment and poor motivation is best tackled by improving the practice of diagnostic, formative assessment.
- Classroom dialogue about learning should be focused on enabling students to give thoughtful and reflective comments. Students need to be given more time to think about and express their ideas.
- Students' formative, self-assessment and focused teacher feedback should be diagnostic and aimed at pinpointing how learning can be improved. This process needs to be carried out more rather than less frequently, so that the partnership of reflective practice can strategically build the full range of dispositions necessary for learning how to learn.
- Tasks are best planned when teachers share insights about what makes a good unit of work, and what would constitute criteria for success and be a good way of using assessment processes to improve the learning process on that unit of work. Students' inadequate learning culture can only be improved by finding the time to cultivate the dispositions to make this possible.
- Teachers should use meta-cognition to reflect about why students fail to learn in their classes, so that their present inadequate motivation and deployment of learning strategies can be improved and overcome.

Black & Wiliam's specification for improving learning through assessment would be enriched by adding the systemic analysis of activity theory – that is, by creating whole school or district wide policies and practices that complement those found in subject-specific communities of practice. Therefore, the following bullet point should be added to the list above.

- Assessment for self-regulated learning must be systematically and consistently applied throughout the subject community of practice and the whole school (and district wide).

Black & Wiliam highlight the chicken-and-egg feature of the successful practice of meta-cognition in which pupils can only become accurate at assessing their work and setting new targets if they know the projected learning outcomes for a unit of work and how their performance can be self-monitored in relationship to such outcomes. They argue that this form of practice is best promoted by structuring classroom assessment dialogue around three mutual elements: the present evidence-base for the attainment of pupils; the desired new learning targets; and the learning strategies used to close the gap between the two (see **Figure 2**).

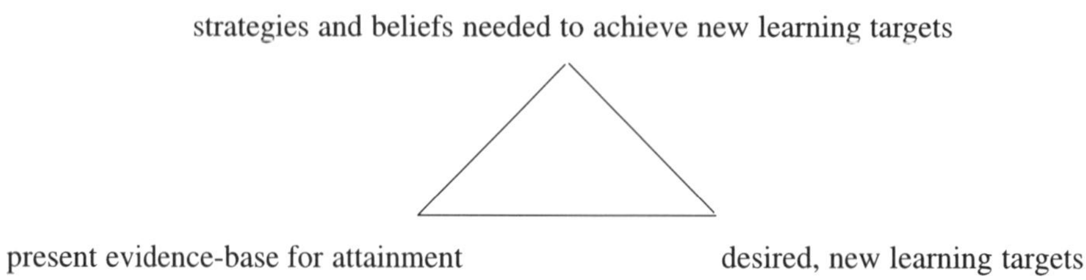

Figure 2

Initiating pupils into this process is not straightforward as it involves dissonance, difficulty and tension; hence the need to cultivate the disposition or intrinsic motivated belief to want to show task commitment for practising meta-cognition without the adverse dominance of negative feedback. Following Aristotle, Zagzebski[51] argues that epistemic virtues, like moral virtues, can only be acquired over time through combining intrinsic motivation to deliberately practice virtue with the example of others who model the virtues. Learning to use meta-cognition also requires years of such deliberate practice by drawing on intrinsic motivated belief and by having self-regulated learning explicitly modelled by significant others like teachers. Spillman's article on differentiation[52] highlights the importance of teachers systematically modelling the necessary repertoire of skills, cognitive processes and character traits to include dealing with fallibility when things go wrong and how to show task commitment to overcome such difficult periods, as this is an inevitable part of engaging with any deep as opposed to surface forms of learning and creativity.

Conclusion

This article has raised issues about the purposes and practices of assessment in art education. In so doing, it comes out strongly in favour of practices that promote and cultivate the dispositions that lead to self-regulated learning and creativity. Adopting such a strategic approach to nurturing self-regulated cognition and developing certain character traits for creativity requires a radical change in the current assessment culture of art education, which predominantly continues to use assessment for alternative and often educationally regressive ends. The critique of current practices of assessment in art education offered in this chapter is built on a variety of sources and arguments to include: Ofsted inspection information that reveals the same weaknesses in art assessment practices as those identified in wider research in assessment; research in two paradigms of cognitive psychology that identify the salient cognitive processes and dispositions that are required to achieve self-regulated learning; research that provides a multi-level analysis of learning to include the Neo-Vygotskian idea of mentor/apprentice relationships that operate in a participation theory of learning; Wittgenstein's philosophy of mind that makes a distinction between following a rule for action and acting in accordance with a rule, and which also exposes the sickness in dualistic thinking and its corollary of a mentalist shadow world of intuition; research that makes up the new sociocultural paradigm of learning and creativity that has established a key role for mentors giving expert instruction for improving learning and creativity, as well as the significance of the duration of time taken to build and deliberately practice the necessary knowledge and skills for achieving excellence; and, finally, work in virtue that sees epistemic and creative reliability as emerging and operating in an analogous way to ethical virtue in that all three require the deliberate acquisition of stable character traits and good habits of mind that go down deep.

The research discussed in this chapter provides the necessary framework from which to build a paradigm for assessment in art that would be consistent with a sociocultural paradigm of art education. The different fields of research provide a clear picture of the salient features and causal factors that would enable students to genuinely flourish at regulating their own learning in relationship to reproducing and transforming mind in culture. Whether art educators will be willing to change their practices in response to the arguments put forward in this chapter is open to doubt. Ofsted inspection findings show classroom practitioners to be unaware of the importance of practising a future-tense approach to assessment predicated on nurturing self-regulated learning. A survey of the literature on assessment and art education would also suggest that many commentators prefer to be mired in the modernist metaphysical stance of the art educator rather than be engaged with a new paradigm of sociocultural thought that aims to enable students to learn how to learn. This makes it difficult to feel confident that the new sociocultural assessment paradigm for art education that is articulated in this chapter will become a norm for future practice.

Notes and references

1. Jay, E, Perkins, D N & Tishman, S (1993), Teaching Thinking Dispositions: from Transmission to Enculturation, *Journal of Theory into Practice*, vol. 32, summer edition, pp. 147–153; see also Efland, A (2002), Art and Cognition, New York: Teachers' College Columbia University, p. 118.
2. Metcalfe, J & Shimamura, A P (eds.) (1996), Metacognition: Knowing about Knowing, London: MIT Press, p. viii.
3. Gombrich, E H (1960), Art and Illusion, London: Phaidon Press.
4. Cunliffe, L (1998), Gombrich on Art: A Social Reconstructivist Interpretation of his Work and its Relevance to Education, *Journal of Aesthetic Education*, vol. 32, no. 4.
5. Gombrich makes this comment in Miller, J (ed.) (1983), States of Mind: Conversations with Psychological Investigators, London: BBC publications, p. 224.
6. Figure 1 is adapted from Blagg, N (1993), Somerset Thinking Skills Course Handbook, Taunton: Nigel Blagg Associates; see also Cunliffe, L (1998), Art and Art Education as a Cognitive Process in R Burden & M Williams (eds.) *Thinking through the Curriculum*, London: Routledge.
7. The lists are compiled from Nisbet, J & Shucksmith, J (1986), Learning Strategies, London, Routledge; Blagg, N *op. cit.*; Perkins, D N & Tishman, S *op. cit.*; Cropley, A J (1997), Fostering Creativity in the Classroom: General Principles, in M Runco (ed.), *The Creativity Research Handbook, Vol. 1*, Cresskill, New Jersey, Hampton Press, pp.83–109.
8. Parsons, M J (1996), The Assessment of Studio Work and Distrust of Language, in D Boughton, E W Eisner & J Lligtvoet (eds.) (1996), *Evaluating and Assessing the Visual Arts in Education*, New York: Teacher's College, Columbia, p. 58.
9. See Hursthouse, R (1999), On Virtue Ethics, Oxford: Oxford University Press for a discussion about why whiz kids find it easier to operate with algorithmic rules as opposed to complex heuristics.
10. Aristotle (1951), The Nichomachean Ethics, in P Wainwright (ed.) *Aristotle: An Anthology*, New York: Odyssey Press, pp. 181–199.
11. See Gruber, H E (1993), Creativity in the Moral Domain: Ought Implies Can Implies Create, *Creativity Research Journal*, vol. 6, 1 & 2; Macleod, J & Cropley, A J (1989), Fostering Academic Excellence, Oxford: Oxford University Press; Code, L (1987), Epistemic Responsibility, London: Brown University Press.
12. Black, P & Wiliam, D (1998), Inside the Black Box, London: King's College.
13. Ofsted reports for art and design are available online from URL www.oftsed.gov.uk/publications.
14. For the contrast between nihilistic forms of creativity and practices of creativity predicated on the future tense, see Steiner, G (2001), Grammars of Creation, London: Faber & Faber.

15. See the summary of art as self-expression in the table reproduced in Clark, G, Day, M & Greer, D (1987), Discipline Based Art Education: Becoming Students of Art, *The Journal of Aesthetic Education*, vol . 21, no. 2.
16. Efland, A, *op. cit.*; see also Harré, R (1983), Personal Being, Oxford: Blackwell, p. 20.
17. Mitchell, S E (1996), Institutions, Individuals, and Talk: The Construction of Identity in Fine Art, *Journal of Art and Design Education*, vol. 15, no. 2, p. 152.
18. *Ibid.*, p. 150.
19. Curtis, R, Weeden, P & Winter, J (2000), Measurement, Judgment, Criteria and Expertise: Intuition in Assessment from Three Different Subject Perspectives in T Atkinson & Claxton, G (eds.), *The Intuitive Practitioner*, Buckingham, Open University Press, p.226.
20. Wittgenstein, L (1958), Philosophical Investigations, Anscombe, G E M & Rhees, R (eds.), trans. Anscombe, G E M, Oxford: Blackwell; Wittgenstein, L (1980), Remarks on the Philosophy of Psychology, vol. 1, Anscombe, G E M & von Wright, G H (eds.), trans. Anscombe, G E M, Oxford: Blackwell; see also Harré, R & Gillett, G (1994), The Discursive Mind, London, Sage Publications, pp.76-77.
21. Cunliffe, L (2005), The Problematic Relationship Between Knowing How and Knowing That in Secondary Art Education, Oxford Review of Education, vol. 31, no. 4.
22. Harré, R (2001), Norms in Life: Problems in the Representations of Rules in D Bakhurst & Shanker, S G (eds.), *Jerome Bruner: Language, Culture, Self*, London: Sage Publications, pp.155-156.
23. Best, D (1985), Reason and Feeling in the Arts, London: Allen & Unwin.
24. Jay, E, Perkins, D N & Tishman, S, *op. cit.*
25. For the factors that need to be calculated for productive risk-taking in gambling, see Perkins, D (1995), Outsmarting IQ, London: Free Press.
26. Owens, T (1995), Bebop: The Music and Its Players, Oxford: Oxford University Press.
27. Gombrich, E H (1960), Art and Illusion, London: Phaidon Press, pp.126–152.
28. For an example of the selective emphasis on risk-taking at the expense of the other dispositions, see Swift, S & Steers, J (1999), A Manifesto for Art in Schools, *Journal of Art and Design Education*, vol. 18, no.1, pp. 7–13.
29. Ash, A, Schofield, K & Starkey, A (2000), Assessment and Examinations in Art and Design in N Addison & Burgess, L (eds.), *Learning to Teach Art and Design in Secondary School*, London, Routledge/Falmer, pp. 134–162; Binch, N (1994), The Implications of the National Curriculum Orders for Art for GCSE and Beyond, *Journal of Art and Design Education*, vol.13, no. 2, pp.117–131; Blaikie, F (1994), Approaches to Secondary Studio Art Assessment in North America, *Journal of Art and Design Education*, vol. 13, no. 3, pp. 299–311; Boughton, D, Eisner, E W & Lligtvoet, J (eds.) (1996), Evaluating and Assessing the Visual Arts in Education, New York: Teacher's College' Columbia University; Karpati, A (1995), Assessment of Art Education in Hungary: Historical Problems in Contemporary Perspective, *Journal of Art and Design Education*, vol. 14, no. 3, pp. 277–288; Schonau, D W (1991), Nationwide Assessment of Studio Work in Dutch Secondary Art Education, *Journal of Art and Design Education*, vol. 10, no. 1, pp. 81–87; Steers, J (1994), Art and Design: Assessment and Public Examinations, *Journal of Art and Design Education*, vol. 13, no. 3, pp. 287–297.
30. *Ibid.*, Ash, Schofield & Starkey, p. 136.

31. Boekaerts, M (1999), Self-Regulated Learning: Where Are We Today?, *International Journal of Educational Researcher*, vol. 31, pp. 445–457.
32. Zimmerman, B J & Schunk, D H (1989), Self-Regulated Learning and Academic Achievement, cited in M Boekaerts (1999), Self-Regulated Learning: Where Are We Today? *International Journal of Educational Researcher*, vol. 31, p. 446.
33. Desforges, C (2001), New Theories of Learning and Their Implications for Assessment, presentation given at the conference of the Association of Assessment Inspectors and Advisors, September 2001.
34. Harré, R *op. cit.*, p. 161.
35. Bereiter, C (1991), Implications of Connectionism for Thinking about Rules, in *Educational Researcher*, vol. 20, no. 3, pp. 10–16; see also Kischner, D & Whitson, J A (eds.), Situated Cognition, London: Lawrence Erlbaum.
36. Strauss, C & Quinn, N (1997), A Cognitive Theory of Cultural Meaning, Cambridge: Cambridge University Press, pp. 53-54.
37. Weisberg, R (1999), Creativity and Knowledge: A Challenge to Theories in R J Sternberg (ed.), *Handbook of Creativity*, Cambridge: Cambridge University Press.
38. Howe, M J A (1999), Prodigies and Creativity in R J Sternberg (ed.) (2001), *Handbook of Creativity*, Cambridge: Cambridge University Press.
39. Sfard, A (1998), Two Metaphors for Learning, *Educational Researcher*, vol. 27, no. 2, pp. 4–13.
40. Black, P & Wiliam, D (2002), Working Inside the Black Box, London: King's College.
41. See Boden, M A (2001), Creativity and Knowledge in E Craft, B Jeffrey & M Leibling, M (eds.), *Creativity in Education*, London: Continuum; Sternberg, R J (ed.) (2001), Handbook of Creativity, Cambridge: Cambridge University Press.
42. Weisberg, R, *op. cit.*
43. Kroeber, A L (1944), Configurations of Cultural Growth, Berkeley: University of California Press.
44. McClelland, D C (1961), The Achieving Society, New York: Van Nostrand; see also Murray, C (2004), Human Accomplishment, New York: HarperCollins.
45. Simonton, D K (1981), Creativity in Western Civilization: Intrinsic and Extrinsic Causes, *American Anthropologist*, vol. 83, pp. 628–630.
46. Ochse, R (1990), Before the Gates of Excellence: the Determinants of Creative Genius, Cambridge: Cambridge University Press.
47. Csikszentmihalyi, M (1999), The Study of Creativity in R J Sternberg (ed.), *Handbook of Creativity*, Cambridge: Cambridge University Press.
48. Engestrom, Y, Miettinen, R & Punamaki, R-L (eds.) (1999), Perspectives on Activity Theory, Cambridge: Cambridge University Press.
49. Engestrom, Y & Cole, M (1997), Situated Cognition in Search of an Agenda in D Kischner & J A Whitson (eds.), *Situated Cognition*, London: Lawrence Erlbaum, pp. 301–310.
50. Black, P & Wiliam, D (1998), *op. cit.*
51. Zagzebski, L (1996), Virtues of the Mind: an Enquiry into the Nature of Virtue and the Ethical Foundations of Knowledge, Cambridge: Cambridge University Press.
52. Spillman, J (1995), Differentiation, *Managing Schools Today*, vol. 4, no. 4, pp.12–14.

Chapter 9: Assessment in educational practice: Forming pedagogized identities in the art curriculum

Dennis Atkinson

Introduction: The Ambassadors

There is a painting by Holbein housed in the National Gallery in London entitled *The Ambassadors*, which has been employed by Lacan and others to illustrate their explorations of identity, representation and meaning. I want to use this picture to begin my study of the discourses in which teachers and students develop and acquire their pedagogized identities, that is to say, their identities as learners and teachers. However, I will provide my own interpretation of Holbein's painting to suit my purpose. The painting is well known. Two richly clothed dignitaries are standing either side of a set of shelves on which are displayed collections of objects and measuring instruments. They look out towards the viewer. In the central foreground, rising from the base, there is a mysterious form which appears as a smudge, a fuzzy image. If the viewer takes up a position to the extreme right of the painting the smudge is transformed and reveals itself to be a representation of a skull. The technical term for this visual manipulation or distortion of form is anamorphosis. It is a technique which interested painters of the period. The interesting point about the painting is that from a frontal perspective this meaningless shape is surrounded by meaning, that is to say, all around the mysterious shape meaning is abundant in the form of recognizable representations. This idea of lack at the centre of a field of meaning, this apparent void in the midst of recognizable form, is something I will explore in relation to assessment practices.

In school art lessons some students produce mysterious images which are difficult to interpret, they are rather like the meaningless smudge in Holbein's painting. That is to say, within the discourses through which we form understanding of representational practice and which constitute assessment criteria, these images are a mystery. But if we are able to change our perspective, if we are disturbed enough to reflect upon the hermeneutic structure of our interpretational discourse there is the possibility of forming a new hermeneutic, rather similar to taking up a different viewing position before Holbein's painting, so that meaning emerges. I shall discuss such disturbance leading to the possibility of a change in perspective in order to effect a more inclusive approach to assessment and, consequently, a radicalization of perceptions of students as learners.

In this rather speculative paper my particular focus will be assessment in educational practices with specific focus upon assessing drawing from observation. In my experience assessing children's or student's artwork has always been a problematic aspect of teaching art in schools. There are some who feel that to even consider assessing artwork is rather pointless because art is concerned with self-expression and we should value equally each individual's form of expression and representation. Others feel that it is possible to assess student's artwork if we select the appropriate criteria and forms of judgement. My purpose in this paper is to consider how assessment as a discursive practice can be considered as an apparatus of visibility and surveillance. I want to discuss how assessment in art practice actually constructs or makes visible both student's and teacher's pedagogized identities. To begin, consider the five drawings below. They were produced in a lesson where the students (age 11-12 yrs) worked in pairs and took turns to make a line drawing of their partner. This is a common drawing exercise in schools in the UK.

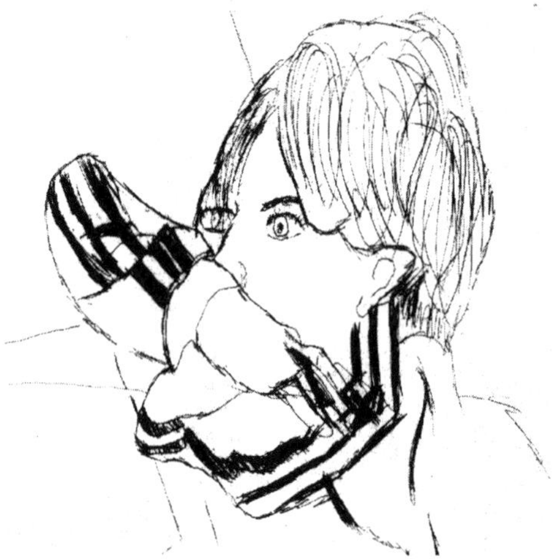

1

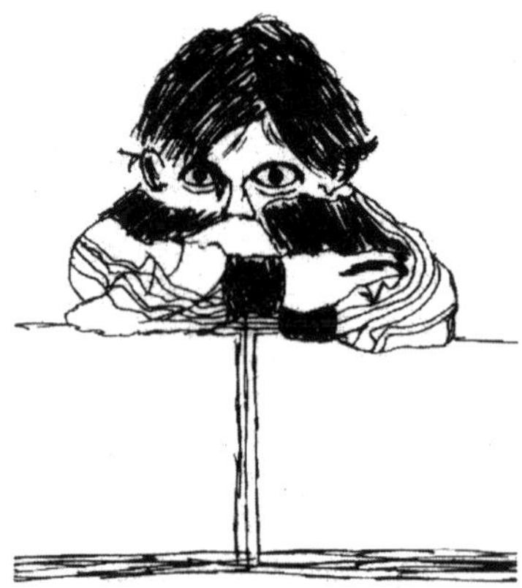

2

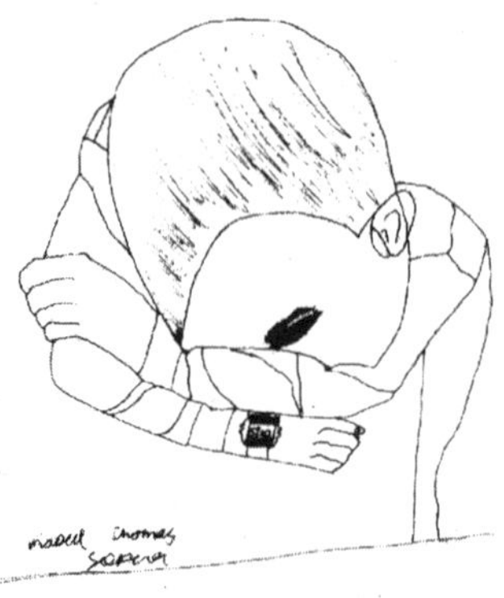

3

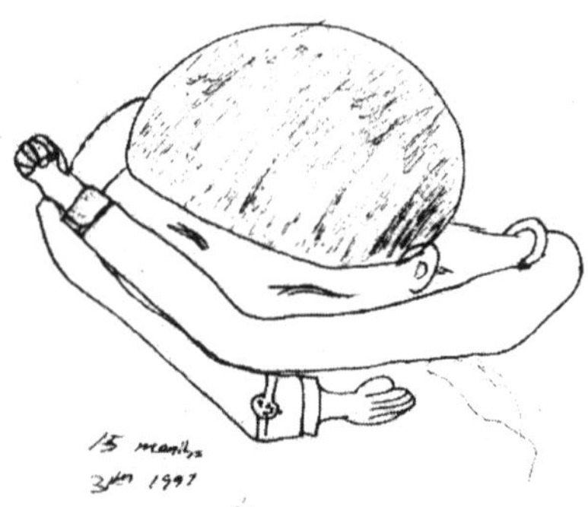

4

Many drawings which students produce are assimilated or recognized within codes of representation through which they achieve meaning. This is not because the drawing reflects a visual correspondence with reality (although we might believe this to be the case) but because the drawing is recognized within accepted representational codes. However, there are some drawings which jar, their form is mysterious and they are frequently regarded as

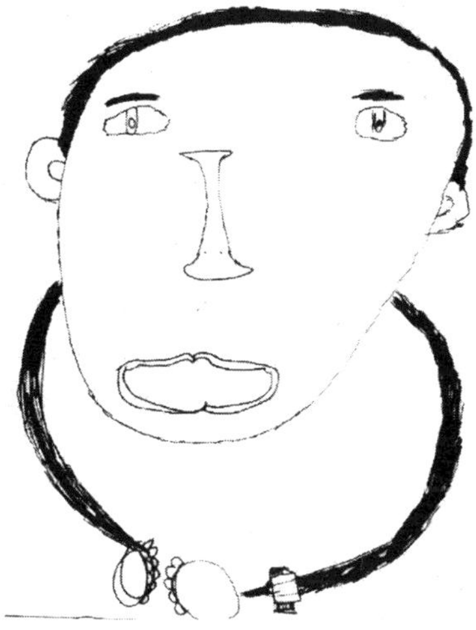

5

poor representations which reflect a lack of drawing ability. The effect of the oddness or the singularity of such drawings upon a student's pedagogized identity is that the student frequently occupies a place of *otherness* in relation to the normative forms of accepted drawing practice. The student becomes what I call a *pedagogized other* of the accepted symbolic order of drawing practice. Referring to Butler, the student becomes a marginalized subject within the specific discourse in which drawing ability is assessed.

> *All identities operate through exclusion, through the discursive construction of a constitutive outside and the production of abjected and marginalised subjects, apparently outside the field of the symbolic, the representable,* ***which then return to trouble and unsettle the foreclosures we call identities*** (my emphasis)[1]

For me it is the drawing in figure 5, the one which troubles and unsettles my foreclosure, which I find interesting in relation to the task of assessment and the subsequent identification of the student as learner.

One possible scenario of assessment might be to regard drawings 1 and 2 as more effective representations than drawings 4 and 5 with drawing 3 lying somewhere between these pairings. Drawing 5 is strikingly different and could be regarded as weak or defective as a representational drawing. A poor representation which indicates that the student responsible for its production could be regarded as less able in drawing practice than the other students. In assessment discourse the drawings represent the subject of practice not simply for other subjects (teachers responsible for assessment) but primarily for other signifiers, that is to say, for the symbolic network of representational codes or discourses of visuality in which the drawings as signifiers have to be inserted to achieve meaning. We may acknowledge the representational forms of drawings 1 and 2 because they can be easily understood within accepted codes of representation. Equally we can marvel at the economy and sophistication of drawing 3, it is indeed a beautiful drawing in which the use of a mainly orthographic system produces a powerful representation of the solidity and positioning of the body.

Drawings 4 and 5 in differing degrees disturb the representational codes we tend to employ when assessing such drawings. However, drawing 5 is so different, so singular, that it is not easily understood and it is likely to be assessed as weak or even child-like in relation to the other drawings. But if we regard this drawing as defective we also, by implication, construct its author's pedagogized identity accordingly. I shall argue there is another way of considering such strange drawings, but first I want to spend a little more time on assessment.

Assessment of students' art practices

There is a central difficulty embedded in the field of art in education. This relates to the difference between discursive frameworks within which we conceive and perceive art practice and the event or the act of practice. This difference mutates into that between a teacher's understanding of art practice gained from his or her work as an artist and the pedagogic requirement to initiate, understand and assess the art practices of students within the institution of art education. Frequently these differences are illustrated by many teacher's open acknowledgement *in theory* of the legitimacy of different ontological (ways of being) and epistemological (ways of knowing) orientations of individuals engaged in art practice and the teacher's imposition, *in practice*, of specific epistemological values which presuppose specific ontological orientations. Thus the outcomes of some practices and experiences are valued more than others. The imposition of value on students' art practices impacts upon the construction of both students' and teachers' pedagogized identities.

Consider the following statement from an assessment discourse about which I have written previously.[2] It is an assessment of student's painting of a building site:

> *Information about the shapes of buildings and machinery which feature in the environment has been observed and recorded but greater analysis is needed in order to represent this accurate*ly.[3]

The following statements are taken from a secondary school art department's assessment policy:

> *To be viewed excellent a student: can clearly visualize and record accurately using appropriate basic elements.*

Some assessment statements on individual students taken from their progress reports state:

> *A is able to record from observation from a wide range of sources with some accuracy.*

> *B is able to record accurately from observation.*

> *C has difficulty recording responses to observations...and needs to use imaging skills including scale, perspective and composition.*

The words *accurately* or *accuracy* suggest that representation is a matter of attempting to achieve a visual correspondence with viewed reality, the purpose of representation is to achieve optical truth. These terms are signifiers which, within the assessment discourse, presuppose a particular ontology and epistemology of visual experience in which the world can be perceived, understood and represented through the representational medium 'as it is'. Information from the world passes directly through the retinal membrane and is directly translated into a graphic form. It is the translation of this perceptual information into a graphic representation which is anticipated as a matter of drawing skill.

The signifier *accuracy* thus presupposes an objective world, which is knowable or perceivable as it is through representational form. This signifier provides the crucial semantic pivot around which meaning is structured in the assessment statements above. A student's pedagogized identity is constructed therefore according to the level of graphic skills which the representational form exhibits. The drawing system which is often viewed as facilitating optical truth is perspectival projection and it is this representational system which often forms the benchmark for determining the representational efficacy or accuracy of an observational drawing and, consequently, in determining a student's pedagogized identity as a subject of drawing practice. Frequently this relationship is cemented by what Bryson (1983, pp.10-11)[4] calls the *natural attitude* towards representation. Put simply this attitude assumes a visual correspondence between the form of objects in the world and the form of objects as represented on the drawing surface, when viewed from a particular position. In the drawings of children and students a drawing's representational form is often assessed according to its degree of natural correspondence with a particular view of the real object.

What I want to do next is to introduce a series of conceptual terms from the work of Jacques Lacan in order to try to theorize how assessment as a discursive practice produces pedagogized identities. I shall draw upon Zizek's interpretation and exposition of key Lacanian terms in order to develop a critical reading of common assumptions concerning the relationship between an observational drawing and its referent in the world.

It is with the notions of inclusion and exclusion in the construction of pedagogized identities as these are formed in assessment practices with which I am concerned. I shall argue that the natural attitude to representation consists of a fantasy which fetishizes students' drawings and the notion of ability. That is to say, that ability is viewed as being *in* the student and *in* the drawing. I will suggest that assessment of observational drawing does not involve comparing the drawing's representational efficacy with an 'actual' view of objects (although this often appears to be the case), but relies upon the fantasy of an objective world which is representable as it is. This is a further fetishistic practice which hides the subjective production of objectivity (see Zizek 1997, p. 97).

Consequently, in assessment practices there is nothing behind or prior to the drawing which is directly accessible (such as a real object) except representational fantasies, that is to say, a consensual system of signifiers, which already precede and go beyond the drawing. For assessment discourses and practices to avoid being dominated by the natural attitude to representation, I argue that it is important to try to pass through this particular representational fantasy in order to establish a more inclusive approach for responding to the semiotic differences of student's representational practices. However, passing through this fantasy does not infer that a place of truth will be attained on the part of the interpreter, but rather a new hermeneutic state whose epistemological foreclosure will, ultimately, be subject to further deconstruction and illumination.

Lacanian terminology[5]

Objet petit a: this can be understood as an object which causes desire, an object which we seek but which we never attain. It is a fantasy object; something which has no existence in reality but which nevertheless structures desire. It can be conceived as a fantasy object which lies beyond symbolization but around which symbolization circles. Attempts to reveal the essence of *society*, *tradition*, *democracy*, *intelligence*, *ability*, in order to expose their hidden kernel of meaning, always in the end fail because such terms are constituted upon an essential lack which is masked by the term itself. Each term can be viewed as constituting a fantasy object, *objet petit a*. The current concern for *standards* is an interesting illustration of *objet petit a* functioning within the politics of educational policy. This term, as Williams[6] shows, when acting as a plural singular, is frequently employed for suasive or consensual purposes. When considered closely, unless specific standards in the sense of an ordinary plural are identified for specific areas of practice, the use of *standards* as a plural singular seems to refer to something universal and unquestionable. Indeed, as Williams tells us, it is difficult 'to disagree with some assertion of standards without appearing to disagree with the very idea of quality.' But the concern for standards in education does not signify an unchanging, universal and permanent referent, for as societies change so do values, and even within specific socio-historical periods there are radical disagreements about standards. Thus this popular term has no essential meaning but develops meaning within specific ideological discourses.

Signifiers such as *standards* and, as I shall show, *ability* are not points of density of meaning, although this appears to be the case, rather they can be viewed as signifiers without essential signifieds. They are conceived and experienced as points of plenitude of meaning[7] but it could be argued they occupy a place of lack. Such signifiers constitute the Lacanian *objet petit a* in the sense that their apparent reference to specific signifieds is created through a fantasy (ideology) object of desire (the need to 'raise standards'). Another way of talking about this is to recognize the relative nature of such discourses within their specific social and historical contexts. In teaching and learning contexts the term *ability* is often used by teachers to identify students' levels of understanding and practice, as though the word signified some inherent property which a student possessed. But considered another way it refers to a particular kind of behaviour which is deemed acceptable or desirable within particular practices and ideologies of teaching and learning. Often in the field of art in education students who are considered to be able drawers are those able to draw in a particular way or, put differently, able to employ a particular representational system. Thus the term *ability* does not identify an essential property but a form of behaviour or practice that is valued within specific paradigms of teaching and learning.

The well-known anecdote recounting the meeting of Zeuxis and Parrahasios provides an illustration of *objet petit a* functioning in the act of interpreting a visual representation. Whilst Zeuxis produced an image of grapes which appeared to fool birds, he is similarly deceived by Parrahasios who has painted a veil on the wall. Zeuxis asks Parrahasios to show what he has painted behind the veil. The key point is that the very 'act of concealing deceives us precisely by pretending to conceal something',[8] and it is this 'something behind', this essence or inner substance, which we seek which constitutes *objet petit a*...because of course there is nothing behind the image, only ourselves, our projections. In the practice of assessing student's drawings it is often the case that we look beyond the drawing to a supposed reality in order to consider the drawing's representational efficacy.

Point de capiton: this term translated into English as 'quilting point' or 'anchoring point' refers literally to an upholstery button, a device which pins down the stuffing in upholstery work. Analogously, Lacan uses the term to discuss how particular signifiers retroactively stitch the subject into the signifying chain. Zizek develops the notion of quilting with reference to the Althusserian idea of interpellation and shows how key signifiers interpolate or hail individuals into subject positions. He describes how meaning is structured through key nodal points[9] or signifiers which articulate the truth of a particular ideological discourse. For example, if discourse concerned with freedom is quilted through communism, a particular structure of meaning will develop, relating to class struggle and so on. On the other hand, if this discourse is quilted through an idea of liberal democracy, a different structure of meaning develops. Zizek[10] argues that what is at stake in the ideological struggle is which of the nodal points, *points de capiton*, will totalize the structure of meaning. The *point de capiton* is thus a signifier which, as a signifier, unifies a given field, constitutes its identity: it is, so to speak, the word which things themselves refer to recognize themselves in their unity.[11] The importance of this term for the constitution of subjectivity and identity is crucial because individuals are interpellated into subject positions through discourses whose structure of meaning is unified by *points de capiton*.

> *The point de capiton is the point through which the subject is sewn to the signifier, and at the same time the point which interpellates individual into subject by addressing it with the call of a master signifier...in a word, it is the point of the subjectivation of the signifier's chain.*[12]

The words *accurately* or *accuracy* as used in the above assessment statements function as Lacanian *points de capiton*. Theorizing the term *accuracy* as a Lacanian *point de capiton* invokes the possibility of a different epistemology and ontology of assessment practice to that produced within the natural attitude to perception and representation. It revokes the natural attitude to assessment in which representation is understood as the direct retrieval of information from the world via the process of perception and offers the possibility of understanding representation as a signifying practice which constructs rather than retrieves perception and reality. The term *accuracy* creates the illusion of a directly accessible world and the illusion of the representational system's ability to retrieve its truth. It is the Lacanian *objet petit a*, a desired object, which lies behind the signifier *accuracy*, not a directly accessible world but only the illusion of such a reality. The desire for representational accuracy, as manifested in the assessment statements above, is therefore driven by two fetishized illusions, one consisting of a belief in an objective world which we can know 'as it is' and the other in a belief in the efficacy of a representational form to make such knowledge available. To push this a little further, it can be argued therefore that the assessment statements are grounded in the fantasy of a directly accessible world and a fantasy of a representational system which can elicit optical truth. If this is the case, students' representational practices and their pedagogized identities as art practitioners are assessed not according to an objective external criterion, such as optical truth, but in Lacanian parlance, according to fantasy constructions (*points de capiton*) which revolve around *objet petit a*; not real objects but objects of desire.

The Real *is that which resists symbolization absolutely*.[13] This is perhaps the most difficult Lacanian concept to describe because, put quite simply, the Real is that which resists or is beyond signification. Nevertheless it has important implications for interpreting phenomena in the context of educational practice and assessment leading to the subsequent formation of students' and teachers' pedagogized identities.

Lacan's use of the term Real fluctuates as it is employed in different ways in his writings in relation to the orders of the imaginary and the symbolic. The most uncomplicated sense of this term refers to brute existence, to a '*hard impenetrable kernel that resists symbolisation*'.[14] For most of the time our experience is understood through language, visual codes and other social structures. But occasionally what we experience goes beyond the symbolic register as Miller states:

> *The Real is a shock of a contingent encounter which disrupts the automatic circulation of the symbolic mechanism; a grain of sand preventing its smooth functioning; a traumatic encounter which ruins the balance of the symbolic universe of the subject.*[15]

Bowie also describes the distinction between the Real and the symbolic:

> *The network of signifiers in which we have our being is not all that there is, and the rest of what is may chance to break in upon us at any moment.*[16]

It is 'the rest of what is' which could be said to constitute the Lacanian Real and which we experience purely as contingent encounters which disrupt our symbolic frameworks. On encountering the Real, Bowie[17] argues that 'the mind makes contact with the limits of its power, with that which its structure cannot structure.' This is an important factor to bear in mind when reflecting upon assessment practices in education.

The eruption of the Real within the symbolic order creates a destabilization of our frameworks of understanding, this is the essential point. Peter Weir's recent film, *The Truman Show*, provides a beautiful illustration of this process. Truman's life (unknown to Truman) is totally constructed by a media mogul, Christo. All the people in Truman's world are actors who play his friends, business colleagues, even his wife. His entire life is lived within a gigantic film set. However, during the film incidents occur, like the crashing to Earth of a large spotlight, which Truman finds totally bewildering, they puncture his understanding and create instability within the symbolic order of his existence

The Real then is that which cannot be accounted for within the symbolic universe, which, when it is encountered, cannot be understood. Although I have spoken of the Real as a disturbance of the symbolic, it is important not to forget that the symbolic order introduces a cut in the Real.[18] The Real is always primary, always there, but is largely overwhelmed by our ideas of reality which are the products of symbolization. Lacan hints at the difference between reality and the Real:

> *It is the world of words which creates the world of things – things originally confused in the hic et nunc of the all in the process of coming-into-being.*[19]

Thus as well as denoting that which lies beyond symbolization, the Real, by implication, refers to that which is lacking in the symbolic order, a foreclosed element, that which is foreclosed by the symbolic and which can never be grasped.

But why is the Real relevant to this paper? Zizek[20] discusses the Real-as-object when describing writing not as signifier but simply as object. Drawing number 5 above could be regarded as a Real object, as something lying beyond our conventional frameworks of understanding. Such drawings disturb the ways in which we understand representation in drawing practice; they puncture the accepted representational codes.

Consequently, we may need to consider and evaluate, not the drawing, but the very discourses and classification systems in which we understand and assess such drawings and students' art practices. We must, as Wittgenstein wrote in his *Remarks on Fraser's Golden Bough*, 'face the error and recognize the truth in it.' This may involve reflecting upon the epistemological frameworks which constitute our understanding and the ontology of a student's drawing practice. Such reflection may present us with possibilities for developing a more inclusive approach to the difference of students' art practices. Such reflections thus disrupt the power-knowledge frameworks of assessment in which students' pedagogized identities are forged and teacher's assessment practices are confirmed.

To return to drawing 5, this can be viewed rather like the smudge in Holbein's *Ambassadors*, in that it appears as a meaningless form in the midst of the discourses in which we understand representational form. Such drawings are, to quote Bryson,[21] '*so generically unplaceable*', however, rather than pathologize the image, we may gain more insight by assessing the lack in our understanding and moving towards a new discursive position, a realignment of discourse and image. This would entail a radical overhaul of the purpose of assessment in art in education and, subsequently, the way in which we understand students' art practices. The consequence of this may lead to what Grossberg[22] identifies as a 'project of constructing a form of knowledge which respects the other without absorbing it into the same…'. The difficulty, as Lacan reminds us, is that

> *The signifier producing itself in the field of the Other, makes manifest the subject of its signification. But it functions as a signifier only to reduce the subject in question to being no more than a signifier, to petrify the subject in the same movement in which it calls the subject to function, to speak, as subject.*[23]

Concluding remarks

In this study I have focused on the difficult practice of assessment. My intention is to expose what might be considered a cultural politics of representation in order to disturb specific assessment discourses in art education which constitute pedagogized identities. I have argued that the construction of pedagogized identity in observational drawing practices is not founded on assessing a student's ability to perceive and represent the world 'as it is'. Rather, such identity is constructed within specific discourses and representational codes which appear 'natural'.

I have argued that particular discursive terms, e.g., *accuracy*, which appear to presuppose an objective world which is accessible through perceptual experience and reproduced in drawing, actually presuppose fantasy objects, *objets petit a*. I have also shown how assessment discourse fetishizes ability as existing *in* the student or *in* the drawing. Consequently, the constructive power of the discourse to produce pedagogized identities goes unnoticed and ability is taken to be a natural capacity. In disrupting the fantasy screen of assessment discourse, the Real-as-object reveals the lack in the discourse and, for a moment, can shift our gaze towards a greater accommodation of the difference of students' art practices.

Perhaps a way forward, as far as the art curriculum is concerned, is to acknowledge the need for order, as constituted by assessment practices, but to strive for a different kind of order. An order whose temporality is heterogeneous, an order which is grounded in a project of difference, an order which values different ontologies of practice, an order where the singular is not reduced to the normative, an order which is grounded in local experience.

A version of this paper was published in the *Journal of Art and Design Education* 20.1, 2001.

Notes and references

1. Butler, J (1993), *Bodies That Matter*, p. 22, London: Routledge.
2. Atkinson, D (1999), A Critical Reading of the National Curriculum for Art in the Light of Contemporary Theories of Subjectivity, *Journal of Art and Design Education*, vol. 18, no. 1.
3. SCAA, (1996), *Consistency in Teacher assessment: Exemplification of Standards*, Hayes, Middlesex: School Curriculum and Assessment Authority.
4. Bryson, N (1983), *Vision and Painting: The logic of the gaze*, pp.10-11, London: Macmillan Bryson provides five principles which, for him, constitute the natural attitude to visual representation. Drawing extensively on his text, I will provide a summary of four of these: 1. An absence of history. The basic visual field is consistent across generations and corresponds to the fixed nature of the optical body. Visual experience is thus universal and transhistorical and it is, therefore, possible to judge along a sliding scale how closely an image approximates the truth of perception. 2. Dualism. The retinal membrane separates the world of the mind from the world of extension. Outside a pre-existent reality flooded with light which is thus reflected inside by a passive specular consciousness. The self is not responsible for constructing the content of consciousness which is formed by the incoming stream of information from outside. 3. The centrality of perception. The natural attitude is unable to account for images which depart from universal visual experience except in negative terms: the painter has misperceived the optical truth or has been able through lack of skill to provide optical truth. 4. Communication. The representational image transports as perfectly as it can to the viewer the artists original perceptual experience.
5. The Lacanian terms I use in this paper arise frequently in Jacques Lacan's text *Ecrits: A Selection.* A very accessible introduction to these terms can be found in Slavoj Zizek's book, *Looking Awry: An Introduction to Jacques Lacan Through Popular Culture* (1991), Cambridge. Mass. London: MIT Press.
6. Williams, R (1980), Keywords, p. 249, London: Fontana/Croom Helm.
7. Zizek, S (1989), *The Sublime Object of Ideology*, p. 99, London & New York: Verso.
8. Ibid., p.196.
9. Ibid., p.87.
10. Ibid., p.88.
11. Ibid., pp. 95-96.
12. Ibid., p. 101.

13. Lacan, J (1988), The Seminar. Book 1. Freud's Papers on Technique, 1953-54, p. 66, trans. J Forrester, New York: Norton: Cambridge: Cambridge University Press.
14. Ibid., p.169.
15. Ibid., p. 13.
16. Bowie, D (1991), *Lacan*, p. 103, London: Fontana.
17. Ibid., p. 105.
18. See Evans, D (1996), *An Introductory Dictionary of Lacanian Psychoanalysis*, p. 159, London & New York: Routledge.
19. Lacan, J (1977), *Ecrits, A Selection*, p. 65, trans. Alan Sheridan, London: Routledge.
20. Ibid., p. 171.
21. Ibid., p. 187.
22. Grossberg, L (1996), Identity and Cultural Studies – Is That All there Is?, p. 103, in S Hall & S du Gay, *Questions of Cultural Identity*, London: Sage.
23. Lacan, J (1986), *Four Fundamental Concepts of Psychoanalysis*, p. 207, trans. Alan Sheridan, London: Penguin.

Notes on contributors

Brian Britton

Brian Britton is head of art and design at a large 11-18 comprehensive in the south-west of England. He studied art and education at Bath and Bristol and has taught art and design for 30 years. He has been a senior moderator for GCSE and GCE A level and was seconded part-time for three years as an advisory teacher for art.

Mika Cho

Dr Mika Cho is a professor of art at California State University, Los Angeles. She studied art and art education in both America and Korea. She is an art educator and visual artist. She teaches both undergraduate and graduate courses in art and design, and training pre- and in-service art teachers in the K-12 teaching credential program. Her research interests are in art-related and educational issues on assessment in teaching and learning, learning style preferences and aesthetics, which are published and presented nationally and internationally. As an artist, she shows her studio work in various galleries and museums.

Leslie Cunliffe

Leslie Cunliffe is a senior lecturer at the University of Exeter where he runs the secondary PGCE art course. He has experience of undergraduate and post-graduate teaching and higher degree supervision. He taught in secondary schools for fourteen years. He has exhibited paintings and drawings at the Royal Academy and the Royal Exchange. His research embraces a range of topics to include empirical aesthetics, cognitive processes and art education, the role of declarative and procedural knowledge in art education, Wittgenstein's philosophy and art education, and virtue approaches to creativity and knowledge. He has published in a wide range of books and research journals.

Tom Hardy

Tom Hardy has worked as an art and design teacher in secondary schools for 24 years and has led art departments in inner-city, mixed, single-sex and selective schools. He trained as a painter at Hornsey College of Art and before teaching he worked as a professional composer and freelance designer. Between 1996 and 2004 he sat on the editorial board of *The International Journal of Art and Design Education* and acted as reviews editor for five years. He is a regular contributor to the *Times Educational Supplement* and has recently edited *Art Education in a Postmodern World* (Intellect Books).

Richard Hickman

Dr Richard Hickman is a senior lecturer at the University of Cambridge. His teaching experience includes thirteen years as a teacher of art and design and as a university lecturer in art education since 1985. He is editor of *Art Education 11-18: Meaning, purpose and direction*, published by Continuum, and *Critical Studies in Art & Design Education* in this series. He is author of *Why We Make Art and Why it is Taught*, also published by Intellect. Richard Hickman is currently director of studies for art history at Homerton College, Cambridge, and course leader for the art and design component of the University of Cambridge PGCE.

Gill Hopper

Gill Hopper is course leader for BA(Ed) Art at the University of Reading. Her research interests are varied and include the history of drawing and its position and role in the primary school; the broad area of women, art and art education, including the experience and self-perception of female art students training to be primary teachers. Her knowledge of art assessment in the primary school draws on her experience as a former primary deputy head teacher responsible for art, her MA in art and design education at the Institute of Education, London, and her current position, which involves the introduction of trainee primary teachers to the teaching of art in the classroom.

Rachel Mason

Dr Rachel Mason is Professor of Art Education at the Centre for International Research into Creativity and Learning at Roehampton University. She has an international reputation for her research and publications in comparative art education and multiculturalism. She is a former president of NSEAD and vice-president of InSEA (the International Society for Education through Art). Her most recent book (co-edited with Larry O' Farrell) is *Issues in Arts Education in Latin America*, and she is editor of the new *International Journal for Education through Art.*

Trevor Rayment

Dr Trevor Rayment is course leader for PGCE Art and Design at the University of Reading. He studied art and art education in Portsmouth and Wolverhampton, took higher degrees in the University of Oxford and the Birmingham Institute of Art and Design and has a doctorate from Oxford Brookes University. He taught art and design in secondary comprehensive schools for 26 years, has been an advisory teacher for art and is a senior examiner for both GCSE and A level. He has published widely in the field, particularly on issues of art education and assessment, and is currently reviews editor of the *International Journal of Art and Design Education.*

John Steers

Dr John Steers was appointed General Secretary of the National Society for Art Education (now NSEAD) in 1981 after fourteen years teaching art and design in secondary schools in London and Bristol. He was the 1993–96 President of InSEA and has served on its executive committee in various capacities between 1983 and the present. He has served also on many national committees and as a consultant to government agencies. He has published widely on curriculum, assessment and policy issues. He is a trustee of the Higher Education in Art and Design Trust and the Chair of the Trustees of the National Arts Education Archive, Bretton Hall. He is also a visiting senior research fellow at Roehampton University, London.

Sylvia Willerton

Dr Sylvia Willerton is a chair of examiners for VCE, GNVQ and GCSE applied art and design qualifications. She has wide experience as a consultant, researcher and adviser with national and regional authorities and councils, including National Council for Vocational Qualifications; Schools Curriculum Assessment Authority; Qualifications and Curriculum Authority and Awarding Bodies. She has been involved in the development and assessment of a wide range of art and design qualifications, both traditional and vocational, and was a teacher for 24 years. Publications have mainly focused on assessment, professional practice and vocational assignments. She studied fine art at St Martins, London, education at Leicester and was awarded a doctorate by Sussex University.

Index

A level 8, 16, 55
achievement 78, 80, 93
activity theory 100–1, 102
Adams, T L 73
Adonis, Andrew 53
Allison, B 22, 77
Aristotle 93, 99, 103
Art in the National Curriculum 31, 32
Arts Council England 19
AS level
  assessment 8, 16, 49–50, 53–6
  introduction of 49–50
  standards 52
  structure 51
  suggestions for improvement 56
  time constraints 51–2
  wow factor, farewell to 50
Ash, A *et al* 98
assessment 7–9
  A level 8, 16, 55
  AS level 8, 16, 49–50, 53–6
  forming pedagogized identities 107–16
  GCSE 8, 11–12, 20, 41–7, 78–9
  GNVQ/VCE 8, 21, 60, 61–7
  primary education 7, 27
    basis for 30–2
    historical perspectives 27–30
    under National Curriculum 32–8
  re-evaluation 77–8
    approaches to 78–9
    issues arising 79–80
    purpose 80–4
    the way forward 84–5
  role in nurturing self-regulated learning 89, 103–4
    current situation 93
    learning theory and assessment 99–103
    meta-cognition 89–93
    Ofsted reports 93–4
    past and current misconceptions about 94–9
  secondary education; *see also* A level; AS level; GCSE; GNVQ/VCE
    conclusion 22–3
    context for 11–12
    developments since 2000 16
    Ofsted reports on 93–4
    orthodoxy 12–14
    research 16–22
    translating policy into practice 15–16
  teacher training 8, 69–74
assessment criteria
  AS level 49
  GCSE 11–12, 13, 15–16, 20, 41–4
  GNVQ/VCE 61, 66
Assessment of Performance Unit 17
Assessment and Qualifications Alliance 23
Atkinson, D 19, 20
attainment 101, 102
  GCSE 41–4
  Key Stage 3 80
  primary education 33, 35–6

Barone, Tom 81
Barrett, Maurice 20, 51
Barton, J & Collins, A 70
Bennett, G 19, 20
Best, David 38, 97
Binch, Norman 13
Black, P & Wiliam, D 100, 101–2
Blaikie, F *et al* 19, 21
Blunkett, David 53
Boekaerts, M 98
Boswell, Tim 61
Boughton, D 15
Bowie, D 114
Broadfoot, P 62
Bryson, N 111, 115
Butler, J 109

California State University 69, 72
Callaghan, James 11
Canada 20, 21

Capey, John 64–5
Centre for Art Education and International Research 17, 19–20
child-centred education 29, 30
Cizek, Franz 28
Clarke, Kenneth 56
Cochrane Collaboration 18
Cockroft Report 65
Cognitive Abilities Tests 42–7
cognitive strategies 90–3, 103
connoisseurship 15, 61, 77, 84
contextual studies 14
continual assessment 60, 82
coursework
A/AS level 16, 49, 52
GCSE 15, 22–3, 42–3, 44, 45–6, 89
craft skills 14
creativity 38
critical studies 14
CSE 11, 13, 52
Curtis, R 96–7

Darwin, Charles 79
De Eça 19, 21
Dearing Report 63, 64–5
Department for Education and Skills 18, 65, 67
Desforges, C 99
Dewey, John 54
diagnostic assessment 79
differentiation 103
drawing
assessment 107–11, 115
GCSE 14
primary education 28, 29, 30, 36

Ecclestone, K 59
Edexcel 50
Education Reform Act 1988 30, 80
Eisner, Elliot 12, 29, 54, 61, 77, 81
Elbow, P 73
Erwin, T D 71
ethics 93
evaluation 30, 31–2, 78, 84, 90–3; *see also* group evaluations
Evidence for Policy and Practice Information and Co-ordinating Centre 18–19
examinations 78
AS level 49, 52–3, 55
GCSE 14, 15, 42–3, 46–7
GNVQ/VCE 61–4, 66
primary education 30
examining boards 11, 15, 20, 63
exemplar material 20, 53
expert performance 99–100
expression 34, 84
external assessment 21, 22, 101
vocational awards 60, 61, 62, 63, 64, 65, 66, 67

Finney, John 83
formative assessment 31, 79, 98, 101, 102

GCE Applied (Double Award) 59, 66, 67
GCE O level 11, 13, 15
GCSE 8, 11–12, 20, 41–7, 78–9
GCSE Applied (Double Award) 59, 66
GCSE Grade Criteria Working Party for Art & Design 11–12
gender bias 21
Gentle, Keith 30–1, 32, 37
GNVQ 8, 21, 59–67
Gombrich, E H 89–90, 98
grading 78
Graham, Duncan 53
Graham, Martha 54
Grossberg, L 115
group evaluations 81
Gulbenkian Report 30, 31–2, 37

Hargreaves, Eleanor 83–4
Harré, Rom 96, 99
Higher Education Funding Council for England 18
Hillage, J *et al* 18
history element 14
Hodgson, Ann 54
Holbein, Hans 107, 115
Howe, M J A 100

imagination 34, 84
Institute of Education 18, 54
intuition 84, 96–7
inventiveness 34
ipsative assessment 79, 98

Jay, E *et al* 97
Jessup, Gilbert 61–2

Kaprow, Allan 54
key skills 61, 65, 66
Kroeber, A L 100

Lacan, Jacques 107, 111, 112–15
learning outcomes 33
learning theory 99–101
lettering 14
Lowenfeld, V 84
Lucas, Geoff 65

McClelland, D C 100
McClune, Billy 55
Macgregor, R N *et al* 19, 20
mark schemes 15, 54–5
materials 28–9, 30, 34, 35
measuring 78
Mellon Lectures 89
mentors 100, 103
meta-cognition 89–93, 94, 97, 99, 101, 102–3
Miller J A 114
Mitchell, S E 95
modcration 15, 66, 67
Modernism 28, 95, 96, 98, 104
modularity 16, 49, 50, 51, 55
monitoring, primary education 32
Morgan, Margaret 32
Mozart, W A 100
mural design 14

National Council for Vocational Qualifications 59, 61, 62, 63, 64
National Curriculum for Art and Design 20, 27, 30, 32–3, 34, 35
National Curriculum Council 12, 53
National Education Research Forum 18
National Foundation for Educational Research 22, 42
National Society for Education in Art and Design 17, 19, 51, 53
National Strategy for Systematic Reviews in Education 18
Netherlands 21
New Art 28

Nietzsche, F 93
norm referencing 42, 55–6, 95, 101
NVQ 60, 61, 65

Ochse, R 100
Ofsted 22–3, 37, 66, 93–4, 103–4
Organisation for Economic Co-operation and Development 17
orthodoxy 12–14

painting 14, 28
Parker, Charlie 98
Parsons, M J 91
participation theory 100
Pasmore, Victor 51
pedagogized identities 9, 107–16
Pedras, M J 71
photography 14
Picasso, P 100
plagiarism 14
Plowden Report 29, 30
portfolios 21, 85
  AS level 53
  trainee teachers 8, 69–74
  vocational awards 65, 66, 67
Portugal 21
pottery 14
Price, Eddie 12–13
primary education 7, 27–38
printmaking 14

Qualifications and Curriculum Authority
  AS level 49, 50, 51, 55, 56
  GCSE 12, 14
  primary curriculum 27, 33, 35, 36–7
  research 19, 22
  vocational awards 65, 67
question papers, changes in 14; *see also* examinations

Rayment, T 19, 20
Reid, Bill 55
research 17–20, 22–3
  case for basing policy on 16–17
  summary of 20–1
Research Evidence in Education Library 18
Richardson, Marion 28

risk-taking 21, 54, 97–8
Roehampton University 17, 19
romantic paradigm 95
Ross, Malcolm 36, 79–80, 81–2

Sabol, F R 19, 21
schemes of work 27, 33, 36–7
Schön, P A 61
School Curriculum and Assessment Authority 12, 63
School Curriculum Development Committee 12
School Examinations and Assessment Council 12
School Examinations Council 12
Schools Council 17
Secondary Examinations Council 11
self-assessment 98, 102
  GCSE 79
  Key Stage 3 20
  primary 35, 36, 37
self-expression 28, 29, 95, 107
self-regulated learning 9, 89, 91–2, 98–9, 100, 102, 103–4
Serota, Nicolas 51
Simonton, D K 100
Simpson, A 28–9
sketchbooks 50
Smith, Ralph 7
Social Science Research Unit 18
Spillman, J 103
Steers, John 51
Strauss, C & Quinn, N 99
summative assessment 31, 98, 101
syllabuses 13–14

target setting 37
Tattersall, Katherine 23
Taylor, Rob 51
teacher training 8, 36, 69–74
teaching and learning, effect of assessment 12–14, 15, 22–3, 54, 83, 101
terminal tests *see* examinations
testing 78
theatre design 14
thinking skills 90
Thistlewood, D 16
timed tests *see* examinations
Tomlinson report 22, 59, 67

United States 21

VCE 59, 65–7
Visual Arts Achievement Tests 21
Vocational A levels 16
vocational education 16, 21, 59–67

Weir, Peter 114
Weisberg, R 100
Wicks, Malcolm 55
Willerton, S 19, 21
Williams, R 112
Wittgenstein, L 96, 97, 103, 115
Wolfe, Alison 61, 65

Zagzebski, L 103
Zimmerman, B J & Schunk, D H 98
Zizek, S 111, 113, 115